BRIGHT IDEAS

Inspirations for MATHS

Published by Scholastic
Publications Ltd,
Marlborough House,
Holly Walk,
Leamington Spa,
Warwickshire CV32 4LS

© 1991 Scholastic
Publications Ltd

Written by Beryl Webber
and Jean Haigh
Edited by Juliet Gladston
Sub-edited by Catherine
Baker
Designed by Sue Limb
Series designed by Juanita
Puddifoot
Illustrated by Juanita
Puddifoot and Liz Preece

Designed using Aldus
Pagemaker
Processed by Pages
Bureau, Leamington Spa
Printed by Ebenezer Baylis
& Son, Worcester

**British Library Cataloguing in
Publication Data**
Webber, Beryl
    Maths. - (Inspirations).
    1. Mathematics
    I. Title II. Haigh, Jean III. Series
    510

ISBN 0-590-76403-9

CONTENTS

INTRODUCTION

Mathematics

The Great Debate on education in England and Wales was initiated by James Callaghan in October 1977. In a speech at Ruskin College, Oxford, he expressed the view that the educational system was failing to equip school leavers to keep pace with the demands of modern industry, with all that this implied for the success and productivity of Britain itself. He suggested that if schools were unable or unwilling to meet the demands of modern society, it might be necessary to impose on them a national core curriculum.

The growing concern about standards of education, including the mathematical attainment of children in our schools, led in 1978 to the Government setting up the Cockcroft Committee of Inquiry into the teaching of mathematics in primary and secondary schools. The Cockcroft Report (Mathematics Counts, HMSO) was published in January 1982. It gave prominence to examples of good teaching and learning in schools.

Following the publication of the Cockcroft report, many of its recommendations have been implemented.

• Mathematics co-ordinators have been appointed in most primary schools.
• In-service education has been provided by national and local groups.
• Diploma courses and higher degree courses have been made available to many teachers.
• HMI have written a series of reports entitled *Curriculum Matters*. One of these reports, *Curriculum Matters 3: Mathematics from 5 to 16* (1985), sets out a framework for schools to use when they are developing their own mathematics programmes.
• Mathematics resource centres have been opened in most Local Authorities.
• Large numbers of advisory support staff have been appointed.

The 1989 Education Reform Act introduced the National Curriculum, which is now to be taught in all maintained schools in England and Wales. As teachers specialising in mathematics education during this period of development and change, we have spent time considering this evolution and have rationalised our thinking on the basis of evidence from debates, discussion, observation and in-service education. This has influenced our philosophical stance with regard to mathematics education. We believe that children are active learners, not passive sponges absorbing directed knowledge. They should take responsibility for their mathematical development and understanding. Teachers are the facilitators in this process.

Our aim in writing this book is to share our ideas and experiences of mathematics in the primary school, and to relate these to recent developments, particularly as regards the National Curriculum and assessment. We have included games, activities and investigative tasks that have been successful with children in the classroom. As the title 'Inspirations' suggests, we believe that mathematics is a creative activity to be enjoyed for its own sake, as well as being a tool for use in everyday life. This is reflected in the aims of teaching mathematics as defined by HMI in *Curriculum Matters 3: Mathematics from 5 to 16.*

Aims of teaching mathematics

• Mathematics as an essential element of communication. For mathematics to be a form of communication, children must be able to interpret it, to decide on its reasonableness and to identify the processes involved.
• Mathematics as a powerful tool.
Mathematics is used as a tool in everyday life, in industry and in society. When used in this way it is not the method that is important but the result; the mathematics is secondary to the information it reveals. For example, counting stock in a supermarket is not an end in itself; the important thing is what the totals tell the staff. Should they order more stock? Will the stock go out of date before it is likely to be sold? Have any of the special offers increased sales?
• Appreciation of relationships within mathematics.
The beauty of mathematics is the way the parts relate to each other to make a whole: for example, fractions, decimals, division and multiplication are all required to understand percentages. Mathematics can become very disjointed in children's eyes as they struggle with various routines and fail to see the wondrous interrelatedness of the subject. For example, work with number patterns can help to establish the links between the three, six and nine times tables.
• Awareness of the fascination of mathematics.

By exploring number patterns or just playing with numbers, children can become fascinated with them. They may see, for instance, the beauty of square numbers. This fascination will encourage them to enquire further into mathematics and not to be put off by its seemingly dry and abstract nature.

• Imagination, initiative and flexibility of mind in mathematics.

The development of technology and its use in primary schools has given children opportunities to be more creative in their mathematical thinking. Floor turtles and LOGO can be used to develop ideas of angles, direction and logic. The calculator can free children's minds and let them show creativity and imagination in their mathematics. Traditional pencil and paper methods were developed as being the most speedy way available, at the time, to compute. The children's own methods can now be encouraged, as when using a calculator these methods are likely to be appreciably faster, less tedious and more accurate. This allows the children to find their own way through problems and helps them to develop creativity and flexibility of mind. For example, costing out the class day trip becomes possible, and tasks like this allow children opportunities to think for themselves.

• Working in a systematic way. *Curriculum Matters 3: Mathematics from 5 to 16* suggests that children need to think clearly, reflect on

what an activity entails and consider which strategies are possible. They must check the reasonableness of a result, and interpret it. For example, discovering in how many ways ten pence can be made up needs to be approached in a systematic way. It is also quite reasonable to repeat a calculation or use a particular checking method.

• Working independently. Children need to have faith in the accuracy of their own work. Using a calculator can help with this, as it means that children will need to check with the teacher less often. This encourages independence of thought, and can free children to take an interest further than they would have been inclined to do before; for example, taking a number pattern on past the first few terms.

• Working co-operatively. The introduction of investigative work and real problem solving gives children scope for planning and discussing mathematical work. This type of open-ended approach is better undertaken in small groups where discussion and co-operation are vital. Participating in games also provides opportunities for socialisation and collaboration.

• In-depth study in mathematics.

Flexible timetables and attractive mathematical resources in the primary school give children opportunities to spend more time exploring ideas and using apparatus creatively for their mathematical development. For example, many children are prepared to spend hours investigating Pascal's triangle or the Fibonacci sequence, using mathematical resources such as Multilink, calculators or a Binostat.

• Pupils' confidence in their mathematical abilities.

An opportunity to work together generating ideas, exploring the potential of mathematical resources and talking about their findings gives children far more confidence in their mathematical ability than, for example, completing a page of sums when their sense of place value is rather hazy.

Classroom approaches

The Cockcroft Report identified six classroom approaches which give opportunities to meet the wide range of aims in teaching mathematics. 'Mathematics teaching at all levels should include opportunities for:
• exposition by the teacher;
• discussion between teacher and pupils and between pupils themselves;
• appropriate practical work;
• consolidation and practice of fundamental skills and routines;
• problem solving, including the application of mathematics to everyday situations;
• investigational work.'
(*Mathematics Counts*, paragraph 243).
These points are developed more fully in Chapter 6.

Elements of learning

The elements of learning we have identified are knowledge, conceptual development and skills. Some or all of these elements are part of any mathematics lesson. For each activity in the chapters which follow we have identified the elements embedded in the tasks.
• Knowledge is the factual content of what is taught. In mathematics as in any other subject, there is a vast body of knowledge which must be sifted through. Schools need to be highly selective when planning what is to be taught.
• Conceptual development refers to the generalisations which are usually arrived at through the process of abstraction from many discrete examples.
• Skills are competencies which we learn in order to perform a task. Once learned these need to be practised regularly for short periods to keep them sharp.
Teaching and learning together form the mathematics curriculum.

The National Curriculum

The National Curriculum for mathematics was introduced in September 1989 for all five-year-old children in maintained primary schools in England and Wales.
The introduction of the National Curriculum has meant that teachers are required to plan, manage, assess and record children's learning with reference to the statutory programmes of study, attainment targets and statements of attainment. In this book, we aim to help teachers feel confident with the mathematical content and language of the National Curriculum. We have included an extensive glossary of mathematical terms, many of which are mentioned in the National Curriculum statements of attainment.

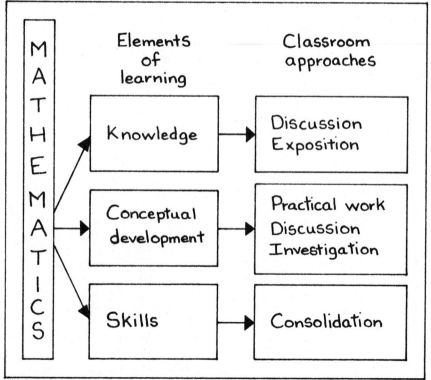

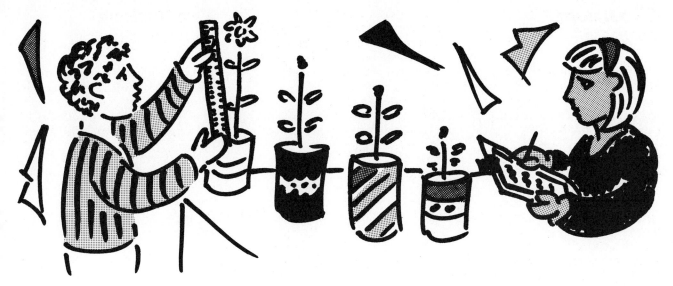

The National Curriculum has a clear structure; the programmes of study are the basis of the teacher's planning, the attainment targets sum up the curriculum content and the statements of attainment are the modules of assessment.

The attainment targets of the National Curriculum for mathematics can be grouped according to the aspect of mathematics on which they focus; numbers, algebra, measures, shape and space and data handling. The processes of mathematics, which are required in order to solve problems and to investigate relationships, should play a part in all mathematical experiences. The activities included in this book follow this basic rule and include opportunities for using and applying mathematics.

Mathematics is also involved in other areas of learning and experience, and Chapter 6 of this book identifies opportunities to develop mathematics from other subjects and to use mathematics as a starting point for cross-curricular activities.

We have included in Chapters 1 to 5 a selection of activities that reflect the attainment targets. They can be used to support the children's mathematical learning but are not sufficient to form a complete programme of study. The activities in each chapter are arranged in three broad age ranges, which approximately reflect the National Curriculum Levels 1 to 3, 3 to 5 and 4 to 6. We have also identified the appropriate number of children for each activity. We have included a range of activities spanning the learning elements of knowledge, conceptual development and the learning or practising of skills. Generally few resources are required, and some of the activities are supported by the use of photocopiable pages. Where appropriate we have suggested further linked developments. These may be particularly useful in extending the experience of the mathematically able child.

The attainment target chart on page 135 shows the relationship between the activities and the National Curriculum. Each activity is identified by a number to denote the chapter in which it occurs and its position within that chapter.

The chapter on assessment and record keeping is intended to support mathematical teaching and learning. It forms the basis for turning an interpretation of the National Curriculum into classroom reality.

We hope that you will find this book useful, supportive and enjoyable and that it will enable you to extend the mathematical experiences of the children in your class. We wish you every success with your mathematics and would remind you of paragraph 2.5 of Section A of the National Curriculum Non-statutory Guidance, which states: 'Mathematics is not only taught because it is useful. It should also be a source of delight and wonder, offering pupils intellectual excitement and an appreciation of its essential creativity.'

CHAPTER 1

Number

This chapter focuses on the topic of number, which has traditionally formed a major part of the primary mathematics curriculum. Children need to develop a sound understanding of all aspects of number and number operations in order to handle everyday adult life effectively. This cannot be achieved by following predetermined rules for which there is no conceptual basis. In the past, children were often taught standard algorithms which, to them, operated in mysterious ways. Now, teachers are trying to encourage a greater understanding of the nature of number and a wide range of strategies to solve numerical problems.

BACKGROUND

Working with numbers

We use numbers in a variety of ways in our environment. Telephone numbers and bus route numbers are purely descriptive; these are called nominal numbers. Other numbers go a step further and also give an indication of order, for example, house numbers. These are called ordinal numbers. These numbers do not imply that there are equal steps between each number and the next, or that there is a zero position in the order. The numbers which represent shoe sizes and dates do imply equal intervals and an order, but they still have no position for zero and cannot be operated on arithmetically. The only number scales that can be manipulated by using arithmetic operations are ratio scales, which have a zero position plus all the qualities of the other three scales, including ordinality and equal intervals. Ratio scales include metric measurements.

A further confusion often exists between number tracks and number lines. Number tracks depict discrete quantities in an order.

| 1 | 2 | 3 | 4 | |

Number lines show continuous quantities that have a position for zero.

0   1   2   3   4

This gives us the opportunity to use arithmetical operations by counting on or back.

The development of number concepts requires a range of skills. These include the identification of an element in a set and of one-to-one correspondence. These skills are fundamental to the understanding of number and are a prerequisite for arithmetical operations.

Skills required for understanding number

• Sorting – objects sharing a common attribute are grouped together.

• One-to-one correspondence – this is necessary before counting can begin.

• Counting – matching number names in one-to-one correspondence to a set of objects.

• Ordinality – ordering according to position.

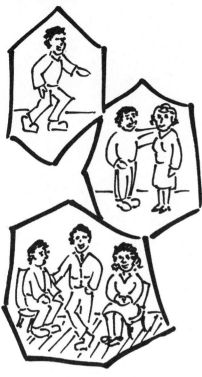

• Cardinality – identifying sets with the same number of members.

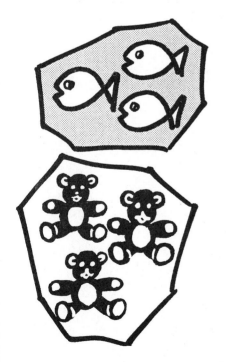

• Conservation – recognising that number is conserved whatever the arrangement of the members of the set.

• Symbol recognition – recognising the abstract number symbols and relating them to the sound of the number words.

123
One Two Three

• Language – all the above points should be developed within the framework of mathematical language; for example, sort, match, same, more, fewer, together, different, smallest, largest, least, most, and so on.
• Zero – this can either denote an empty set or be used as a place holder.

O balloons 702

• Place value – the position of a digit indicates its value, for example 7, 73 and 741 each assign a different value to the digit 7.

13

Number operations

The main ways of thinking about the four number operations, addition, subtraction, multiplication and division, are listed below:

• Addition – combining two or more sets.

• Addition – counting on from an identified point.

It is not until children can 'count on' that they can really be said to be using addition.

• Subtraction – taking away objects from a set.

=2 trees

• Subtraction – working out the difference between two sets.

difference = 3 trees

• Multiplication – adding equal sets.

2p + 2p + 2p = 6p

5 Cokes

+ = 6

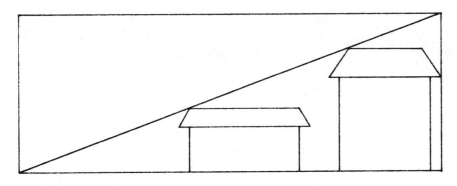

- Multiplication – enlargement.
- Multiplication – arrays.

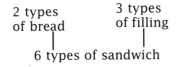

2 types of bread   3 types of filling

6 types of sandwich

NB It is important to note that although we say $3 \times 2 = 2 \times 3$, in fact they are equivalent, not equal. Three cats with two eyes each are not the same as two cats with three eyes each!

- Division – sharing amounts equally between a given number of sets.

- Division – establishing how many sets of a given number can be made.

How many cats can have three fishes each?

- Fractional parts — one third can represent one whole divided into three parts.

(One share is one third of a cake.)

One third can represent a share of a number that is divisible by three.

(One share is one third of six cakes.)

One third can represent a share of a number less than three.

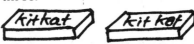

(One share is one third of two KitKats.)

One third can represent a share of a number not divisible by three.

(One share is one third of eight apples.)

One third can represent a share of three.

(One share is one third of three bananas.)

One third can represent a share of a number less than one.

(One share is one third of half a bottle of Cola.)

Chapter structure

This chapter includes activities that support the learning of the three main aspects of number, that is, notation, operations and estimation. Many of the activities require the children to use and apply their knowledge of number, to investigate and to communicate their findings.

ACTIVITIES

1. Insect families

Age range
Five to eight.
Group size
Pairs or small groups.
Objective
To conserve numbers six to nine (conceptual development).
What you need
Photocopiable pages 138 and 139, thin card, adhesive, scissors.
What to do
Mount pages 138 and 139 on thin card and cut along the black lines to make a pack of 16 cards. Play a 'Happy Families' game making sets of cards which show the same insect.

Further activities
Play a 'Pairs' game with the insect cards, matching cards with the same number of insects. Order the cards in sets.

2. Carpet tiles

Age range
Five to nine.
Group size
Pairs or small groups.
Objectives
To recognise halves and quarters of squares and rectangles. To explore different ways of dividing whole shapes (conceptual development).
What you need
Pre-cut 4 × 4 squares, coloured pencils, backing paper, adhesive.
What to do
Stick the pre-cut squares on to backing paper. Choosing two different coloured pencils, the children should find different ways of colouring eight of the smaller squares (half of the 'carpet') to make an interesting pattern. They should colour the small squares completely.

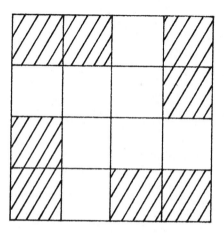

They can now investigate different ways of colouring four squares (a quarter of the carpet), and experiment with different sizes of carpet; for example, 2 × 3, 4 × 3 or 6 × 6.

3. Patch the square

Age range
Five to eight.
Group size
Pairs or small groups.
Objective
To make whole numbers from halves and quarters (knowledge).
What you need
Photocopiable page 140 (you may need several copies of this), scissors, adhesive, backing paper.
What to do
Cut out the halves and quarters from page 140 and let the children find as many different ways as possible of making a whole square from the halves and quarters. The completed squares can then be stuck on to backing paper.

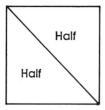

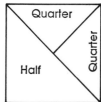

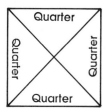

How many ways can the children make two whole squares?

4. Hexagons

Age range
Five to eight.
Group size
Individuals.
Objective
To practise making ten by using addition (knowledge; skills).
What you need
Photocopiable page 141, counters.

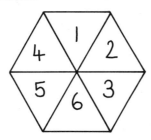

What to do
Ask the children to investigate ways of placing two, three or four counters on the numbered hexagon so that the counters cover numbers which total ten.

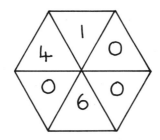

Children can write their own numbers in the blank hexagon and investigate ways of making a number of their choice.
Further activities
Investigate ways of making the highest or lowest total with different numbers of counters.

5. Up and down

Age range
Five to eight.
Group size
Individuals.
Objectives
To practise addition, subtraction and ordering numbers (skills).
What you need
A set of digit cards from zero to ten.
What to do
Shuffle the cards and arrange them in a line face up on the table.

Ask the children to find the nine and place it below the other cards. They then choose a card with a value which is more than nine and place it second. Next they choose a card which is less than the second card and place it third. They continue placing cards with numbers which are, alternately, more or less than that on the previous card, until all the cards have been placed.

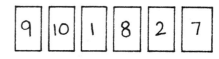

Further activities
Change the pattern rules by using a sequence such as more, more, less, less.

6. Number track

Age range
Five to eight.

Group size
Individuals.

Objectives
To investigate the totals of and differences between pairs or triples of ordered numbers (conceptual development).

What you need
Strips of squared paper, scissors, calculators.

What to do
Number a strip of squared paper beginning with zero.

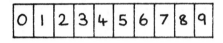

Ask the children to cut off pairs of numbers and investigate their totals and differences using a calculator. They should look for patterns in the totals and differences.

0	1	Total → 1
		Difference → 1

2	3	Total → 5
		Difference → 1

The children could make another strip and cut out different pairs (there will be single numbers left over at either end). Investigate totals and differences again.

1	2	Total → 3
		Difference → 1

3	4	Total → 7
		Difference → 1

Repeat the process again, this time cutting out number triples. Find the difference between the largest and the smallest number.

3	4	5	Total → 12
			Difference → 2

Further activities
Number some strips in different ways, for example:

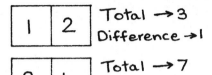

10	9	8	7

1	3	5	7

10	20	30	40

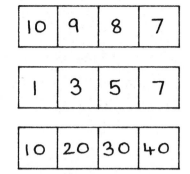

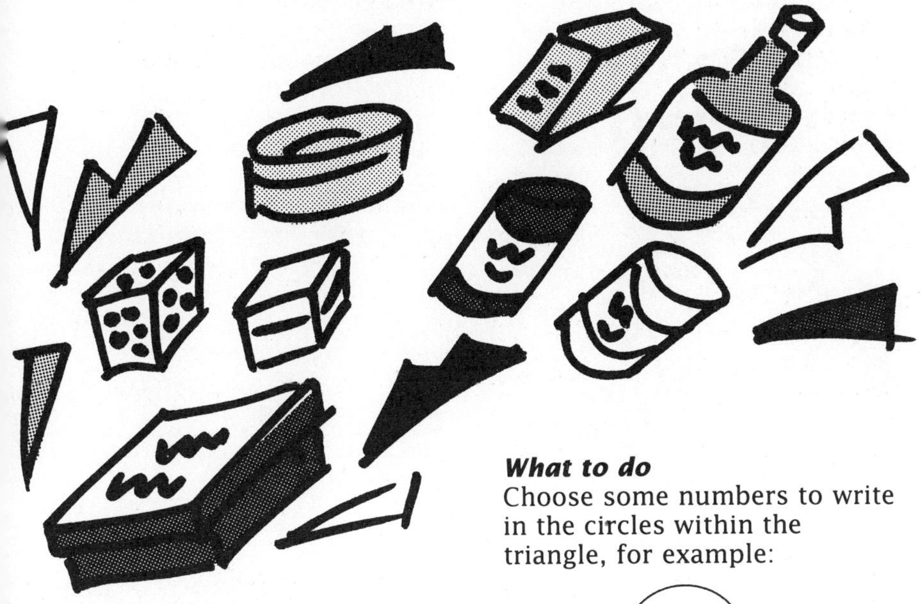

7. Numbers triangles

Age range
Five to eight.
Group size
Individuals, pairs or small groups.
Objective
To investigate adding numbers with a calculator (skills).
What you need
Calculator, copies of photocopiable page 142.

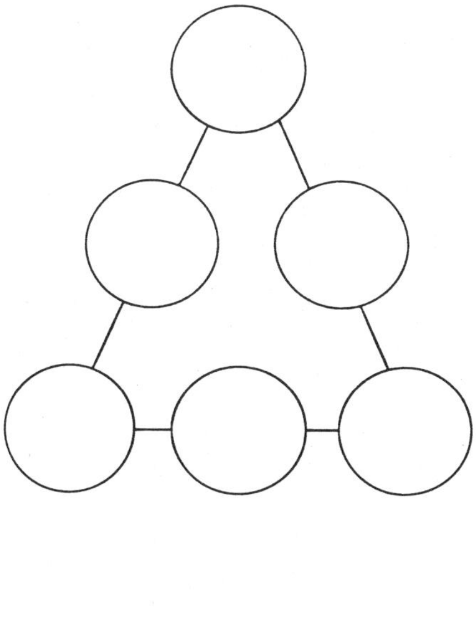

What to do
Choose some numbers to write in the circles within the triangle, for example:

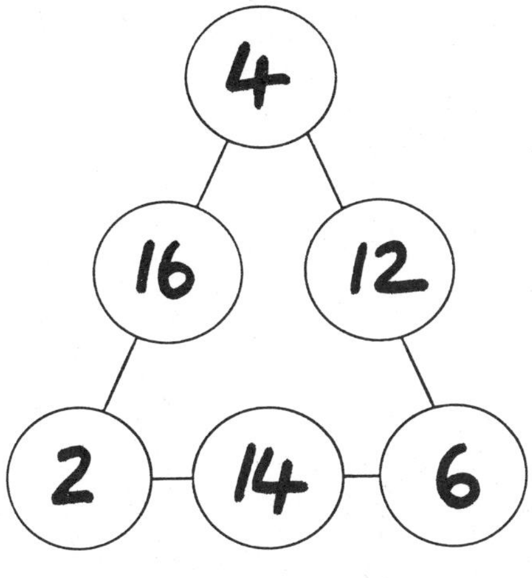

The children can then investigate the totals of the sides using a calculator.

What happens if they add five to all the numbers? Or take away one? What happens if all the numbers are even, or odd?

8. Shopping basket

Age range
Five to eight.
Group size
Whole class.
Objective
To practise estimating numbers of objects to ten (skills).
What you need
A large shopping basket, empty food packages.
What to do
One child puts several packages into the basket and secretly counts how many there are. The other children estimate the number of packages. The first child indicates how 'hot' or 'cold' the estimates are. Let several children have a turn.

9. Balloons

Age range
Five to eight.
Group size
Pairs or small groups.
Objective
To estimate objects to ten (skills).
What you need
Drawing materials, adhesive, scissors.
What to do
Ask each child to draw or paint a large balloon and to put up to five spots on it. They then cut out the balloons. Each child joins with a friend and they estimate how many spots there are on both their balloons together.

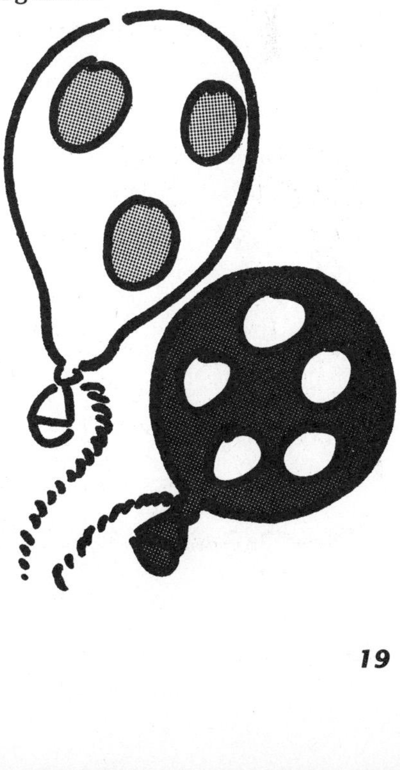

Each child joins with another friend and estimates the number of spots again. Now two pairs join together and estimate the number of spots on their four balloons. They can make a picture using the four balloons.

10. Zeros and ones

Age range
Seven to ten.
Group size
Individuals.
Objective
To use the knowledge that the position of a digit indicates its value (knowledge; conceptual development).
What you need
Calculators.
What to do
Tell the children that they should only use these keys on their calculators:

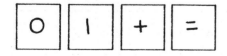

They must use these keys to make the calculator display 21.

They should make a note of which keys they pressed and in what order.

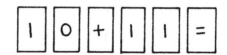

Ask them to find ways of making the calculator show 45, 55, 121 and 210. Then they could choose different numbers to make.
Further activity
Ask the children to choose different keys to work with in a similar way.

11. Fraction jigsaws

Age range
Seven to ten.
Group size
Individuals, pairs or small groups.
Objectives
To recognise and understand simple fractions (conceptual development).
What you need
Photocopiable page 143, scissors, pencils, paper.

What to do
Ask the children to cut out the squares on page 143. They can then re-form them into squares. They should draw round the individual pieces of the completed squares to show what their solution looks like (or transfer the solution on to dotted paper). They should make all the jigsaws in the same way. Ask the children to label each jigsaw piece with the fraction of the base square that it represents.

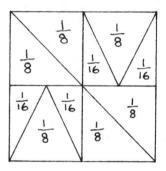

Further activities
The children could make some different fraction jigsaws of their own.

12. Mowing the lawn

Age range
Seven to ten.
Group size
Individuals.
Objective
To find common fractions of a given amount (knowledge).
What you need
Squared paper (1cm), coloured pencils.
What to do
Ask the children to draw a rectangle of 12 squares (to represent a lawn). On Monday they mow half of the lawn. They can colour this amount red. On Tuesday they mow a quarter of the lawn, and colour

this part blue. On Wednesday they mow one sixth of the lawn, and colour this part green. On Thursday they mow one twelfth of the lawn, and colour this part yellow. They should now have mown the whole lawn in four days.

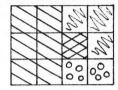

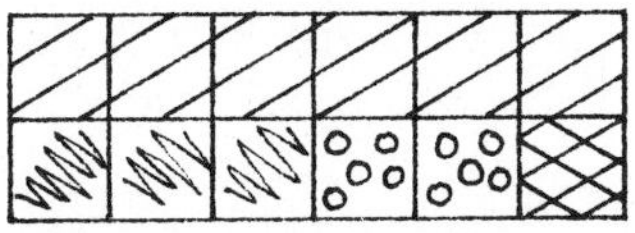

Ask the children to compare their lawns with those of their friends. Next ask the children to do a similar thing with a lawn of 18 squares and the following mowing programme: on Monday half of the lawn is mown; on Tuesday a third of the lawn is mown and on Wednesday one sixth of the lawn is mown.

Discuss with the children what they notice about the fractions.

24 Squares
Monday ⅓
Tuesday ¼
Wednesday ⅙
Thursday ⅛
Friday 1⁄12
Saturday 1⁄24

30 squares
Monday ½
Tuesday ⅕
Wednesday ⅙
Thursday 1⁄10
Friday 1⁄30

Further activity
Let the children try to make a mowing programme for a lawn made up from 36 squares.

13. Fives

Age range
Seven to ten.

Group size
Pairs or small groups.

Objective
To investigate adding and/or subtracting with totals up to 100 (skills).

What you need
Calculators.

What to do
Using the set of numbers 1, 2 and 5 the children should make as many other numbers as they can, either by adding or by subtracting.

$$5 + 1 = 6$$
$$5 + 2 = 7$$
$$2 + 1 = 3$$
$$5 + 2 + 1 = 8$$
$$5 - 1 = 4$$
$$5 - 2 = 3$$

They can choose two more numbers between 10 and 20 to make a set of five numbers altogether, and investigate the numbers that can now be made.

Further activity
The children can investigate how many more numbers can be made if they can also multiply and divide.

They should now choose another set of five numbers that will give them as many different answers as possible.

14. Snakes and ladders

Age range
Seven to ten.

Group size
Pairs or small groups.

Objectives
To use multiplication facts and to recognise multiples (knowledge).

What you need
1-100 number square (numbered from bottom left to top right), coloured counters, die.

What to do
Each player uses a counter as a playing piece. Everyone starts at one and takes it in turn to throw the die, moving their counters the corresponding number of squares.

If they land on a multiple of five, they should move the counter forwards to the next multiple of five. If they land on a multiple of seven, they should move the counter backwards to the last multiple of seven.

Further activity
The children can make up their own rules for moving backwards and forwards.

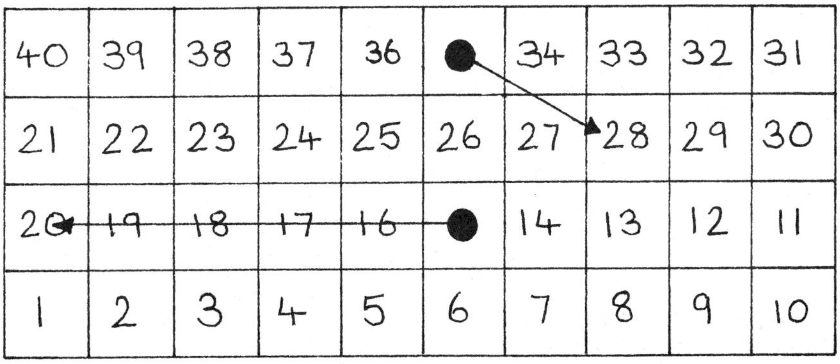

40	39	38	37	36	●	34	33	32	31
21	22	23	24	25	26	27	28	29	30
20	19	18	17	16	●	14	13	12	11
1	2	3	4	5	6	7	8	9	10

15. Cover the multiple

Age range
Seven to ten.
Group size
Pairs or small groups.
Objectives
To multiply three single figures together and to recognise multiples (skills).
What you need
Photocopiable page 144, 40 counters (20 of one colour and 20 of another), three dice.
What to do
The children take it in turns to throw the three dice. They then multiply the numbers together and place their counters over the square which shows the answer. If the square is already occupied, they cannot place the counter. If they throw three ones then they should have another go. The winner is the player who covers four numbers in a straight line – horizontal, vertical or diagonal.

16. Calculator chains

Age range
Seven to ten.
Group size
Individuals.
Objective
To use a calculator to investigate numbers (skills).
What you need
Calculators, two dice.
What to do
Draw this number chain:

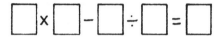

The children roll two dice and put one of the numbers in the first box and the other in the last box. They can choose numbers to put in the other three boxes so that the chain is correct. The children should check the chain with a calculator.

The children draw the chain and roll the two dice again. This time they can put the numbers in any of the boxes. They should make the chain correct and check it with a calculator.

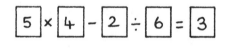

Further activity
The children should draw the chain again, and roll the two dice. Ask them to multiply the numbers shown and write the answer in either the first or the last box. Then they can roll the dice again, and multiply these numbers, putting the answer at the other end of the chain. Finally, they should make the chain correct by adding the intervening numbers, and check with a calculator.

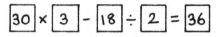

17. Stepping stones

Age range
Seven to ten.
Group size
Pairs or small groups.
Objective
To practise adding numbers mentally (skills).
What you need
Photocopiable page 145, counters.
What to do
The children take turns placing a counter on any number. Only one counter may go on any stepping stone at a time. As they play, the children must keep a running total of all the numbers covered. The player who makes up the total 31 is the winner. If a player makes the total go over 31 he or she loses the game.

18. Place the numbers

Age range
Seven to ten.
Group size
Individuals.
Objective
To investigate placing numbers to a given criterion (skills).
What you need
Photocopiable page 146, pencils.
What to do
Give each child a copy of photocopiable page 146.

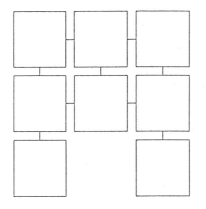

Ask them to use the numbers one to eight, placing one of them in each box so that the numbers in each line add up to 12.

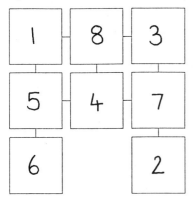

Ask the children to investigate different ways of solving this problem.

Further activities
The children can investigate ways of making the lines add up to 12 using the following diagram and the numbers one to eight.

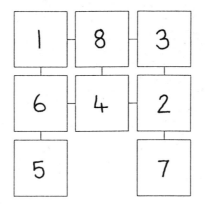

19. Decimal jigsaw

Age range
Nine to thirteen.
Group size
Pairs or small groups.

Objectives
To recognise the value of decimal numbers and to use decimal notation (conceptual development; skills).
What you need
Photocopiable page 147, scissors.
What to do
Ask the children to cut along the thick black lines on page 147, and remake the jigsaw, noting the position of the decimal numbers.

The children can investigate the totals of and differences between the numbers on the jigsaw pieces. They can then investigate the differences between the numbers in the rows and columns.
Further activity
Ask the children to make their own decimal jigsaw using numbers between 0 and 0.1, giving the numbers to three decimal places.

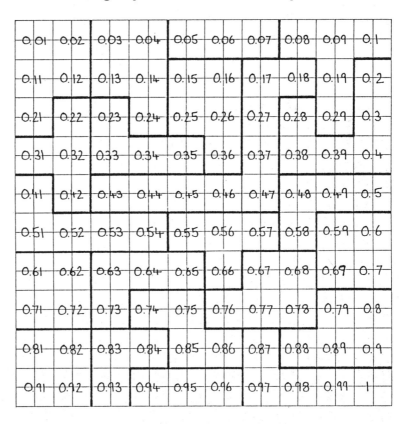

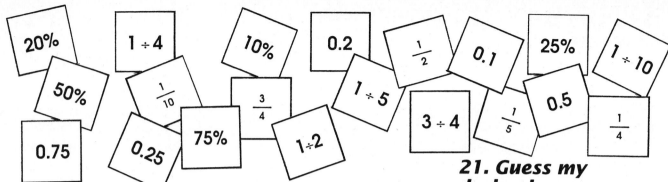

20. Fraction families

Age range
Nine to thirteen.
Group size
Pairs or small groups.
Objective
To recognise equivalence between fractions, decimals and percentages (knowledge).
What you need
Photocopiable pages 148 and 149, scissors.
What to do
Mount pages 148 and 149 on to thin card and cut along the black lines to make a set of playing cards. The children can use the playing cards to play a 'Happy Families' or 'Pairs' game.

Further activities
The children can make a second pack of cards showing the divisions of £1, 1 metre, 1 litre and 1 kilogram.

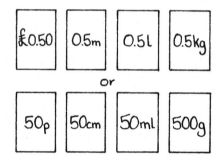

21. Guess my decimal

Age range
Nine to thirteen.
Group size
Pairs or small groups.
Objectives
To place decimal numbers on a number line and to order decimal numbers (conceptual development).
What you need
Several blank number lines, calculator.
What to do
One member of the group secretly enters into the calculator a decimal number between two chosen numbers such as one and five. He or she tells the others to make up their number lines between the chosen numbers. The others make guesses about what the secret decimal number is, and the leader says whether their guesses are too large or too small. Play continues until the number is guessed. The player who chose the secret number is given a score corresponding to the number of guesses taken to get the secret number. Play continues until every member of the group has had a turn at choosing a decimal number. The player with the largest score is the winner.

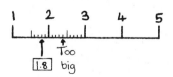

$\frac{1}{2}$	1÷2	0.5	50%	$\frac{2}{5}$	2 ÷ 5	0.4	40%
$\frac{1}{4}$	1 ÷ 4	0.25	25%	$\frac{3}{10}$	3 ÷ 10	0.3	30%
$\frac{1}{5}$	1 ÷ 5	0.2	20%	$\frac{4}{5}$	4 ÷ 5	0.8	80%
$\frac{1}{10}$	1 ÷ 10	0.1	10%	$\frac{7}{10}$	7 ÷ 10	0.7	70%
$\frac{3}{4}$	3 ÷ 4	0.75	75%	$\frac{9}{10}$	9 ÷ 10	0.9	90%

$\frac{3}{4}$ of 16 $\frac{2}{3}$ of 18 20% of 60 $\frac{1}{3}$ of 36 2% of 600 =12

Further activity

The children can try a similar activity restricting the distance between the two chosen numbers to one and using decimal numbers with two decimal places.

22. Brackets

Age range
Nine to thirteen.
Group size
Pairs or small groups.
Objective
To investigate operating with numbers using +, −, ÷ and × with squares, square roots and brackets (conceptual development).
What you need
Cards as shown below, calculators.

| 10 | 2 | 3 | 5 |

| + | − | ÷ | × |

| (|) | $\square^2$ | $\sqrt{}$ |

What to do

Investigate making different answers using all or some of the cards, for example:

(10 − 2) ^{2} × 3 = 192

(5 + 2 × 3) ÷ 10 = 2·1

23. Maze

Age range
Nine to thirteen.
Group size
Pairs or small groups.
Objectives
To calculate fractions and percentages of amounts and to recognise equivalences (skills).
What you need
Photocopiable page 150, calculators.
What to do
The children can use the calculator to help them find a route from 25% of 48 to 2% of 600, moving only on squares showing equal amounts.
Further activity
Ask the children to use a 4 × 4 grid to make a decimal and percentage maze for their friends. They should use a calculator to help them.

24. Units digit

Age range
Nine to thirteen.
Group size
Individuals.
Objectives
To recognise patterns in multiplication and to use the units digit as a method of checking (knowledge).
What you need
Calculator.
What to do
Ask the children to write out the multiplication tables, writing down only the units digit of each answer.

$1 \times 3 \Rightarrow 3$ $2 \times 3 \Rightarrow 6$ $3 \times 3 \Rightarrow 9$
$4 \times 3 \Rightarrow 2$ $5 \times 3 \Rightarrow 5$ $6 \times 3 \Rightarrow 8$
$7 \times 3 \Rightarrow 1$ $8 \times 3 \Rightarrow 4$ $9 \times 3 \Rightarrow 7$

Do this for all the tables up to nine. What patterns do the children notice?

Ask them to make a table showing the multiplications which give a three in the units column.

1×3 7×9 3×1 9×7

Next they can make tables for all the digits zero to nine.

Which digits can be made in the greatest number of ways? Which can be made in the least number of ways?

The children can then try these sums:

$48 \times 6 = 28\square$

$27 \times \square = 135$

$3\square \times 4 = 148$

$1\square \times \square = 133$

Let the children make up some missing digit sums for their friends.

Resources

Calculators
Digit cards showing digits from zero to ten
Operation cards showing brackets, square, square root and +, −, ÷, ×
100 squares
Dice
Counters
Number lines
Multilink
Scissors
Adhesive
Paper
Squared paper
Thin card
Coloured pencils.

CHAPTER 2

Algebra

Algebra can be defined as the generalisation of numerical relationships. For example, the terms of the series of numbers 1, 2, 4, 8 can be generalised by the algebraic expression $2n_{(n-1)}$.

The abstract nature of algebra can make it inaccessible to young children. The number system is in itself an abstraction, and algebra goes one stage further, as it is an abstraction of the number system.

Children are used to dealing with concrete materials; for example, Multilink cubes, plastic toys and coloured beads. They use them to develop ideas and concepts of our number system. For example, the sets shown below can all be represented by the abstract number four.

Numbers can be further abstracted and described in algebraic terms. For example, the series of numbers 2, 3, 5, 9 can be represented by the abstract algebraic expression $2n_{(n-1)}-1$.

BACKGROUND

Children learn to use algebra by taking a situation from the concrete, through the numerical to the algebraic. This is what happens when investigating the size of the border around a central square, as shown below.

By experimenting with this situation in concrete form, using cubes to represent the squares, children will see that there are four corner cubes and therefore the expression must contain 'plus four'. This relates to the number pattern 8, 12, 16.... But this is not the whole story. The concrete situation clearly shows that there are more cubes to account for.

Each side of the border also contains a number of cubes equal to the length of the side of the central square. This can be called length 'n'. There are four of these in each border. This means that the expression must also contain 4n.

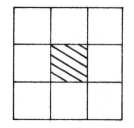

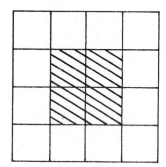

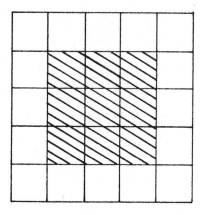

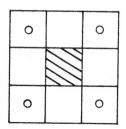

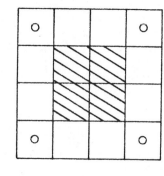

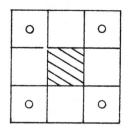

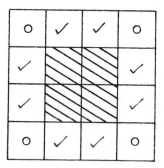

It is important that children develop all three ways of portraying number patterns in their mathematical exploration, and early experiences should include patterns of number bonds, patterns in place value, patterns of multiplication and division, patterns of equivalence and specific number patterns.

$$0 + 5 = 5$$
$$1 + 4 = 5$$
$$2 + 3 = 5$$
$$3 + 2 = 5$$
$$4 + 1 = 5$$
$$5 + 0 = 5$$

Therefore, the full algebraic expression is $4n + 4$ which can be simplified to $4(n + 1)$. This should now be checked using the third example:

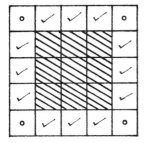

Numerical check

First example: 8 cubes
Second example: 12 cubes
Third example: 16 cubes

$4(n + 1)$ where $n = 3$
$4(3 + 1) = 4 \times 4 = 16$

Concrete check

Four dotted cubes and four lots of three ticked cubes totals 16 cubes.

In order to become proficient at using algebraic skills, children need experience of working with number patterns, unknown quantities and graphical representation.
• Number patterns are fundamental to mathematical exploration. They can be portrayed numerically, algebraically and geometrically.

Children should be encouraged to describe verbally the patterns that they see which can then be generalised in abstract terms.

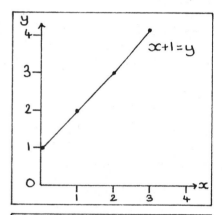

• Algebra involves the manipulation of unknown quantities. A familiar feature of algebra is the expression of unknown quantities as letters or other symbols, for example, $2a + b$, $y = (x)k$, $\blacksquare + \blacktriangle = \bullet$.

Children are often misled into believing that each symbol represents a single, predetermined quantity, so that if you have the equation $a + 3 = 4$, then 'a' will always equal one. They often also believe that letters represent their position in the alphabet, so that $a = 1$, $b = 2$, $c = 3$ etc. They are then further confused when they have to deal with abbreviations such as ab. Children often think this represents 12 rather than $a \times b$, or think of it as $1 + 2$, adding to give an answer of three. Therefore, it is important to avoid focusing too much on equations in the early stages of learning algebra, as this may give the impression that each symbol

represents a single value. Experience of algebraic expressions such as $x + 2$, $a + b$ allows the child to develop the concept of a variable where each symbol represents a possible range of values.

• Graphical techniques are another method of representing algebraic information. Graphs can be used to solve algebraic equations, while clearly demonstrating the variable nature of algebraic terms.

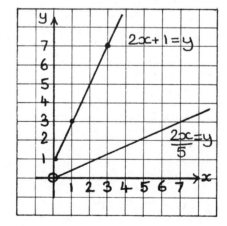

Children need experience of handling co-ordinates in one quadrant, and then later in all four quadrants.

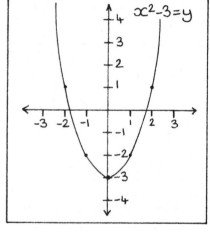

The activities in this chapter are intended to provide children with experiences of concrete situations, numerical patterns and algebraic expressions, including functions and equations. It is important that children are given an opportunity to explore all three modes as necessary.

ACTIVITIES

1. Odd and even snap

Age range
Five to eight.
Group size
Pairs.
Objectives
To practise recognising odd and even numbers and addition to 20 (knowledge; skills).
What you need
Digit cards from zero to nine.
What to do
The children shuffle the cards and deal them all out, and then take it in turns to turn over a card. They try to be the first to call out 'snap' when the two cards that are face upwards add up to an even number.

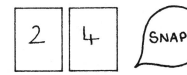

The children should keep the pairs of cards together, and score one point for being the first person to call 'snap' each time.

If the two cards do not add up to an even number, each player returns her card to the bottom of her stack. The children continue playing the game until the greatest possible number of pairs of cards adding up to an even number have been made.

The winner is the player who has collected the most points.

The children can then examine the pairs of cards and investigate the pairs which total an even number.

The children can play the game again, this time calling 'snap' if the totals are odd. Next they can investigate the pairs of cards which total an odd number.
Further activities
Ask the children to design their own game of snap.

$$O + O + E = \text{Even}$$
$$O + E + E = \text{Odd}$$

2. Finding pairs

Age range
Five to eight.
Group size
Pairs or small groups.
Objective
To investigate variables by holding one variable constant while changing another (conceptual development).
What you need
Digit cards from one to six, calculator, coloured pens.
What to do
The children investigate the totals of various pairings of cards. They should choose one card to keep constant and change the second card and total, using the calculator if desired. They should record the pairings and totals.

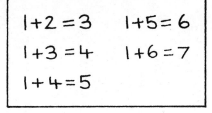

$$1+2=3 \qquad 1+5=6$$
$$1+3=4 \qquad 1+6=7$$
$$1+4=5$$

The children can then alter the constant card and investigate the new pairings.

$$2+1=3$$
$$2+3=5$$
$$2+4=6$$
$$2+5=7$$
$$2+6=8$$

They should continue finding pairings until they have found as many as they can (there are 30 in total).
Further activities
Ask the children to predict how many pairs can be found using digit cards from one to seven.

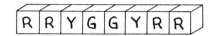

3. Odd and even

Age range
Five to eight.

Group size
Pairs or small groups.

Objective
To investigate the odd and even totals of pairs of odd and even numbers (conceptual development).

What you need
Digit cards from one to six, blank cards, calculator, coloured pens.

What to do
Ask the children to make pairs of cards and to investigate their totals, using the calculator if they wish. They should then write 'O' for odd and 'E' for even on the blank playing cards as appropriate to the sum.

2	+	3	=	5
E	+	O	=	O

They should record their findings. They can then investigate whether two odd numbers always total an even number, whether two even numbers always add up to an even number and what happens when an odd and an even number are added.

+	O	E
O	E	O
E	O	E

Further activity
The children can investigate whether the total is odd or even when three numbers are added.

1	+	2	+	3	=	6
O	+	E	+	O	=	E

Why do they think this happens?

4. Predicting patterns

Age range
Five to eight.

Group size
Pairs or small groups.

Objectives
To investigate continuous patterns and to predict how they grow (conceptual development).

What you need
Multilink or beads.

What to do
Ask the children to create a pattern using five Multilink cubes of alternate colours. They should then try to predict what colour the seventh, ninth, twelfth cubes will be. Ask them to investigate how to find out the colour of any cube in the pattern.

Next, let the children create a pattern using three colours and predict the colours of the tenth, fourteenth and twentieth cubes. Encourage them to explain how to find the colour of any cube in this pattern.

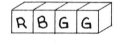

Ask the children to change the pattern and try again. This time they can ask a friend to predict how it will continue, and then check the prediction.

Further activity
The children can make a repeating pattern of cubes using two or three colours and about ten or twelve cubes. They then take away two cubes from the middle of the pattern and ask a friend to guess the colours of the missing cubes.

5. Make fifteen

Age range
Five to eight.

Group size
Pairs.

Objectives
To practise adding numbers to 15. To develop strategies and logical thinking (conceptual development).

What you need
Digit cards from one to nine, counters.

What to do
Ask the children to lay out the cards in order from one to nine. They then take it in turns to place their coloured counters on a card (only one counter is allowed on any one card).

The winner is the first player to occupy three cards which add up to 15.

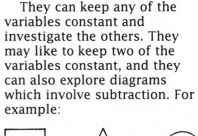

Ask the children to play the game several times, taking it in turns to be the starting player.

Further activity

Ask the children to investigate whether one player will always be able to win. They can also investigate the possible sets of three cards which total 15.

6. Unknown numbers

Age range
Five to eight.

Group size
Pairs or small groups.

Objectives
To use symbols to represent unknown numbers and to investigate addition patterns (conceptual development).

What you need
Photocopiable page 151, calculator.

What to do
Ask the children to write the number ten in all the circles on the sheet. Let them investigate the numbers which need to go in the squares and triangles to make the sums true.

$$\boxed{1} + \triangle{9} = \bigcirc{10}$$

$$\boxed{2} + \triangle{8} = \bigcirc{10}$$

On another copy of the sheet the children should write a different number in all the circles, and again let them investigate ways of making that number. They can then choose a different number to go in all the squares on another copy of the sheet, and investigate sums with that number.

$$\boxed{4} + \triangle{1} = \bigcirc{5}$$

$$\boxed{4} + \triangle{2} = \bigcirc{6}$$

$$\boxed{4} + \triangle{3} = \bigcirc{7}$$

The children can then repeat the activity with a number written in the triangles.

Further activities
Ask the children to investigate other diagrams. For example:

They can keep any of the variables constant and investigate the others. They may like to keep two of the variables constant, and they can also explore diagrams which involve subtraction. For example:

$$\square - \triangle = \bigcirc$$

$$\hexagon + \square - \triangle = \bigcirc$$

$$\hexagon - \square + \triangle = \bigcirc$$

7. Function machines

Age range
Five to eight.
Group size
Individuals.
Objective
To investigate the effect of various functions on a range of numbers (conceptual development).
What you need
Plain paper, calculator, small pieces of card.
What to do
Tell the children that function machines are special: they change numbers. Ask them to write a function, such as +4, on a piece of card, and to try using this function on some numbers; for example, 1, 2, 3, 4, 5 and so on. What do they notice?

Now they can try some other functions on the same set of numbers. What do they notice now?

IN	+4	OUT
1		5
2		6
3		7
4		8
5		9

Ask them to make up some two-stage functions, for example +3 and ×2. What do they notice?

8. Snail trail

Age range
Five to eight.
Group size
Individuals.
Objective
To explore routes following paths of even numbers (skills; knowledge).
What you need
Diagrams similar to the one shown below, counters, coloured pencils.

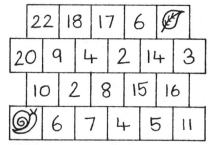

22	18	17	6	🍃
20	9	4	2	14	3
10	2	8	15	16
🐌	6	7	4	5	11

What to do
Ask the children to look carefully at the numbers in the brick wall pattern on the diagrams. Discuss with them any number patterns they can see. When they have found several interesting patterns ask them to find an even route from the snail at the bottom of the wall to the leaf on the top of the wall. The children can use counters or colour the squares to keep a record of their route, and to help them decide whether the numbers are even or not.
Further activity
The children can investigate the number of routes possible from the snail to the leaf.

9. Patterns of nine

Age range
Seven to ten.
Group size
Individuals.
Objective
To investigate patterns of numbers formed by adding nine (conceptual development).
What you need
Calculators.
What to do
Ask the children to set up a constant function on the calculator. To set up a constant 'add nine' function they will probably need to press the following keys:

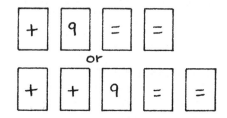

Each type of calculator operates differently, and you may need to experiment beforehand to discover the pattern of keys necessary.

Once the children have set up the constant function, ask them to continue adding nine by pressing the equals key and watch the pattern of numbers as they grow. Ask the children to keep going until they reach 90.

9, 18, 27, 36, 45, 54 ...

Ask the children to investigate the sum of the digits.

$$1 + 8 = 9$$
$$2 + 7 = 9$$
$$3 + 6 = 9$$
$$4 + 5 = 9$$
$$5 + 4 = 9$$

What happens past 90? What happens if they start with a different number and add nine?

4, 13, 22, 31...

Further activity
The children can investigate the sums of the digits from other times tables.

6	12	24	30
↓	↓	↓	↓
6	3	6	3

10. Add a square

Age range
Seven to ten.
Group size
Pairs or small groups.
Objective
To investigate growing patterns (conceptual development).
What you need
Squared paper, coloured pencils.
What to do
Ask the children to colour a square and then, using a different colour, shade four squares adjacent to the first.

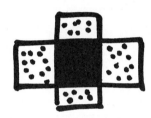

The children should record how many squares they colour each time. They should then repeat the pattern, alternating the colours, but this time using one of the existing squares to provide part of the new pattern. Let them continue the pattern, using only squares which adjoin the existing pattern by a single edge.

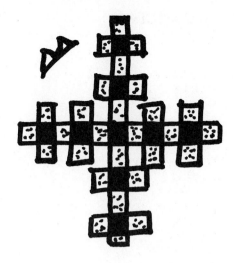

Ask them to record how many squares they add each time. Watch the pattern grow!
Further activity
Ask the children to try repeating the activity using different types of paper, for example, isometric, hexagonal or rectangular.

11. Cube patterns

Age range
Seven to ten.

Group size
Pairs.

Objective
To identify and describe growing patterns (conceptual development).

What you need
Multilink.

What to do
Starting with one Multilink cube the first child adds two more cubes. His or her partner then adds two more cubes to the shape.

The first child then adds another two cubes. The children, taking it in turns, continue for a few more steps. Ask them to describe their growing pattern. Now they can change the rules so that each child can add one more cube each time. That is, the second child adds three cubes, then the first child adds four cubes and so on.

Next they should change the rules again. This time the first child adds three cubes, and his or her partner adds five cubes, the first child then adds seven cubes and so on.

Let the children make up some rules of their own.

12. What's my number?

Age range
Seven to ten

Group size
Pairs.

Objective
To use information to establish unknown numbers (conceptual development).

What you need
A 100 square for each pair.

What to do
One child secretly identifies a number on the 100 square and gives his or her partner two clues to help identify it: 'It is beside...' and 'It is above...'. They should have a few turns each, and then they can change the rules and give different clues: 'It is directly above two numbers that total...' and 'It is beside two numbers that total...'.

What do the children notice about the numbers that have been totalled?

The children can change the rules again, this time giving the difference between two numbers as clues. Does this help them find the secret number?

Further activity
Ask the children to add the three numbers to the left or right and above or below a number. What do the children notice? Can they discover any pattern? Are there any numbers which could be given the same clues?

13. Spirals

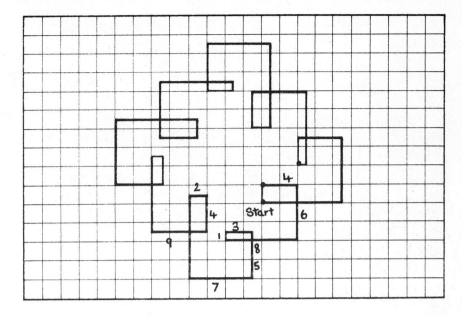

Age range
Seven to ten.
Group size
Pairs or small groups.
Objectives
To investigate growing patterns and to describe them systematically (conceptual development).
What you need
Squared paper, rulers, calculators.
What to do
The children can create two or three growing number patterns, for example:

1, 1, 2, 2, 3, 3...
1, 3, 2, 4, 3, 5...
1, 3, 5, 7, 9, 11...

Ask the children to draw them as spiral patterns on squared paper, changing direction after every number.

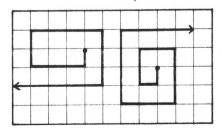

Ask them to describe the patterns in words. They can look at differences between consecutive terms, totals of consecutive terms, triples of terms and odd and even numbers.

Further activity
The children can investigate digital roots of sequences. Ask them to find digital roots by totalling the digits of terms from a number pattern, until they arrive at a single digit.

They can then investigate the spirals of the digital roots. Ask them to choose a starting position on a large sheet of squared paper. It is best if they choose a position somewhere between the centre of the paper and the outside edge. They should draw a line the

length of the first number in their digital root pattern. Then turn clockwise through a right angle and draw a line the length of the second number in their pattern. They should continue, repeating the pattern as necessary until they return to their starting position.

They could investigate the digital root spirals of the times tables (see above). What do they notice about the spirals of the one and eight times tables or the two and seven times tables? Which other patterns are similar to these?

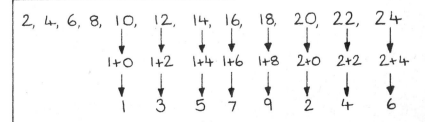

Digital roots of the two times table

2	4	6	8	10	12	14	16	18	20	22	24
				1+0	1+2	1+4	1+6	1+8	2+0	2+2	2+4
				1	3	5	7	9	2	4	6

14. What am I doing?

Age range
Seven to ten.
Group size
Pairs or small groups.
Objectives
To establish functions and to describe them verbally or symbolically (conceptual development).
What you need
A calculator.
What to do
One child chooses a rule for operating on two numbers, which may be as simple or complex as he or she likes. For example, the rule may be, 'Add the first number to the second' or 'Multiply the first number by the second and take away three'. Two numbers are then chosen by the rest of the group. In secret the first child performs the rule, using the calculator, on the two numbers, and writes the result.

First Number	Second Number	Result
2	3	7

The result then becomes the first number and a second number is chosen. The aim of this activity is for the children to discover the rule that has been chosen and to state it.

First (a) Number	Second (b) Number	Result
2	3	7
7	1	8
8	4	33

Rule: multiply the two numbers together and add one or $a \times b + 1$.

Ask the children to change the rule and have another go.

Further activity
The children can play the same game, but this time they should not state the rule. Instead, they can try to choose a second number so that the result, after the function has been carried out, is one.

First Number	Second Number	Result
1	2	3
3	3	6
6	0	6
6	-5	1

is the rule....?

multiply the first number by the second number and add three

15. Package sizes

Age range
Seven to ten.
Group size
Individuals, pairs or small groups.
Objective
To investigate the volumes of packages given the total dimensions (conceptual development).
What you need
Calculator, graph paper.
What to do
The children should investigate the volumes of packages whose total dimensions (length, width and depth) do not exceed 90 units.

Ask the child to find the package size which has the greatest volume and to make a graph of their findings.

Further activity
The children can draw the nets of their packages and construct them from cardboard. Ask them to halve (or double) all of the dimensions of the package and investigate what happens to the volume. Can they explain why this happens?

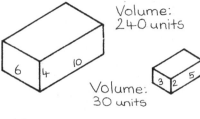
Volume: 240 units
Volume: 30 units

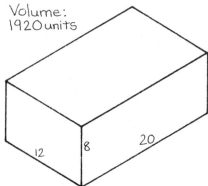
Volume: 1920 units

16. Products

Age range
Seven to ten.
Group size
Pairs or small groups.
Objective
To establish unknown numbers from their products (skills).
What you need
Digit cards from one to twenty.
What to do
Ask the children to lay out the cards in a 5 × 4 grid. One child then secretly chooses two numbers which are on cards that are next to each other, vertically or horizontally. The child should then use the calculator to find the product of the chosen numbers, and then declare the product to the other players. The first player to identify the chosen pair of numbers correctly can remove and keep the cards. This player then chooses a second pair of cards in the same way.

Play continues until all the cards have been won. It may be necessary to redeal the cards in a smaller grid from time to time. The player who collects the most cards is the winner.
Further activity
Ask the children to find the product of three adjacent cards. Again, the players can use calculators to find products and make guesses.

17. Number function machines

Age range
Seven to ten.
Group size
Pairs or small groups.
Objectives
To investigate the inverse operations of addition, subtraction, multiplication and division (conceptual development).
What you need
Photocopiable page 152, calculator, small pieces of card.

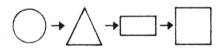

What to do
Ask the children to write some functions on the pieces of card, such as +10 or –4. They should also make another card with the function 'take away the first number' written on it. They can then choose one addition and one subtraction function card (ask them to make sure the addition card has a larger number than the subtraction card to avoid negative numbers).

The children should then arrange the cards on the sheet so that the 'take away the first number' card is last.

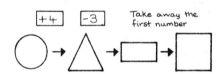

The children can now try putting some numbers through the number function machine. What do they notice?

They should now change the function cards except for the last one. Ask them to try some more numbers and record the results. What do they notice?
Further activity
Ask the children to choose a number and try to create a 'magic' function machine that makes that number.

Now they can try some 'magic' function machines that use multiplication and division.

18	100	55	24	80	26
	14	30	25	16	22	
45	50	10	6	15	60
	30	4	20	35	40	
10	5	15	2	20	25

18. Multiple wall

Age range
Seven to ten.
Group size
Individuals.
Objective
To explore routes following paths of multiples of two, five or ten (knowledge; skills).
What you need
Diagrams similar to the one shown below, calculators, counters, coloured pencils.
What to do
Ask the children what they notice about the numbers in the bricks in the diagram. Ask them to try to find a route from the bottom row of bricks to the top row of bricks moving only on multiples of two. For example:

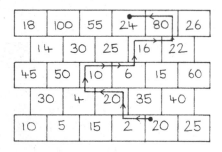

Ask the children to compare their route with their friends' routes. Have they used the same brick to start and/or finish? Are any other bricks the same? Together, the children can look for other routes which contain multiples of two.

Repeat the activity following routes with multiples of five and multiples of ten.
Further activity
Ask the children to design a wall of their own and to make up the rules for following routes through from bottom to top.

19. Special numbers

Age range
Nine to thirteen.
Group size
Pairs or small groups.
Objective
To identify numbers by their properties (knowledge).
What you need
A set of digit cards from zero to 49 for each child.
What to do
Each child lays out the cards in front of herself. Then you ask to see cards such as:

The children can devise some criteria of their own. If a correct card is shown it is turned face down. The first child to have turned over ten cards is the winner.
Further activity
Play the game using two criteria at once. For example:

20. Five in a line

Age range
Nine to thirteen.
Group size
Individuals.
Objective
To use given information to establish unknown quantities (skills).
What you need
Squared paper, calculator.
What to do
Ask the children to cut out some strips of squared paper with five squares on each strip. They should then choose two numbers and write them in the first two squares.

2	5			

The children add the two numbers together and write

the answer in the third square. They should then add the second and third numbers together and write the answer in the fourth square, and continue until the strip is complete.

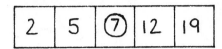

If they are given only the first and last numbers, can the children find the missing numbers?

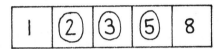

Ask them to investigate what happens when they use different first and last numbers. Can they find a rule to find the missing numbers?

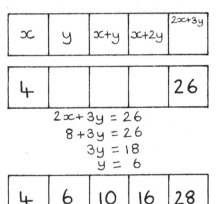

$$2x + 3y = 26$$
$$8 + 3y = 26$$
$$3y = 18$$
$$y = 6$$

Further activity
Ask the children to try to find a rule for other chains of squares.

21. How many factors?

Age range
Nine to thirteen.
Group size
Individuals.
Objective
To investigate the number of factors of numbers (knowledge).
What you need
Calculator, paper, pencil.
What to do
Ask the children to make up a table that shows the numbers 1 to 50 with their factors. For example:

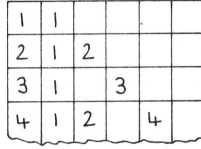

Ask them what the numbers with two factors are called. Which numbers have three factors, and which four factors? What numbers have an odd number of factors? Why?

22. Baseboards

Age range
Nine to thirteen.
Group size
Individuals.
Objective
To investigate making numbers to fit certain criteria (conceptual development).
What you need
Multilink, hundreds, tens and units baseboards.

H	T	U

What to do

The children should place three Multilink cubes on the baseboard to show multiples of five. Ask them to make as many as they can.

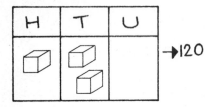

Next they can try to make multiples of three or four, or use four cubes to make square numbers.

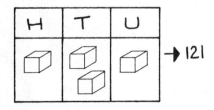

Encourage them to show as many prime numbers as they can.

Let the children choose their own number of cubes and set their own rules.

Further activity

Using three cubes, the children can make a number on the baseboard. Then they should add one more cube. Ask them to investigate the difference between the first and the second number. What is the largest difference? What is the smallest?

23. Area and perimeter

Age range

Nine to thirteen.

Group size

Pairs or small groups.

Objective

To investigate the possible areas of rectangles given the perimeters and vice versa (conceptual development).

What you need

Squared paper, pencils.

What to do

Ask the children to investigate the rectangles that can be made with a perimeter of 36 units and then to look at their areas. What shape gives them the largest area? They should represent this graphically.

Let the children choose an area and investigate the largest and the smallest perimeters possible for rectangular shapes of that area.

24. Number wall

Age range

Nine to thirteen.

Group size

Pairs or small groups.

Objectives

To investigate combining numbers and to explain the result using algebraic symbols (conceptual development).

What you need

Photocopiable page 153.

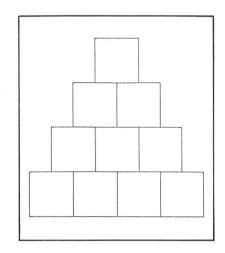

What to do

Ask the children to choose four numbers to write in the bottom row of the wall. They should then combine the numbers by adding them together to form the next row. They can continue this until they reach the top brick.

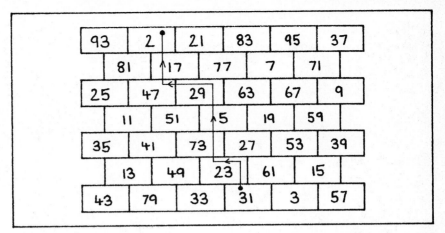

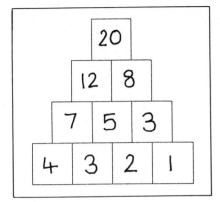

Tell the children to change the order of numbers in the bottom row, keeping the numbers the same. What do they notice?

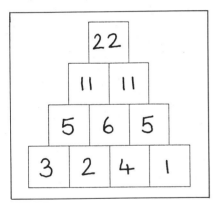

They should try all the different possible orders of the four bottom numbers. What is the largest top number they can make? What is the smallest?

Further activity
Put a different letter in each of the bottom bricks and investigate the wall algebraically.

The children can then use their formulae to establish the top number for any four bottom numbers.

25. Prime wall

Age range
Nine to thirteen.
Group size
Individuals.
Objective
To explore routes following paths of prime numbers (knowledge; skills).
What you need
Diagrams similar to the one shown below, calculators, counters.

93	2	21	83	95	37
81	17	77	7	71	
25	47	29	63	67	9
11	51	5	19	59	
35	41	73	27	53	39
13	49	23	61	15	
43	79	33	31	3	57

What to do
Ask the children what they notice about the numbers in the bricks. Ask them to try to find a route from the bottom row of bricks to the top row of bricks moving only on prime numbers, as shown in the example at the top of the page.

Ask the children to compare their route with the route found by one of their friends. Have they found the same route? Did they start or finish on the same prime number? The children can then work together to discover other prime routes.

Further activity
Ask the children to find other prime numbers. They may wish to use a calculator to help them. The children could then use these prime numbers to make up another prime number puzzle; for example, a cross-number puzzle where the solutions are all prime numbers.

Resources

Calculators
Digit cards
Counters
Multilink
Hundreds, tens and units baseboards
Threading beads
100 squares
Plain paper
Squared paper
Graph paper
Isometric paper
Card
Pencils
Rulers.

CHAPTER 3

Measurements

Measurement is the application of number to the physical world. Traditionally it has taken up a large proportion of the available classroom mathematics time. However, it is only one aspect of an already rich curriculum.

Much time is also given to measurement in the science curriculum, and it is important that the experiences of measurement gained through mathematics and through science are linked and co-ordinated. This is also true for measurement encountered as part of the art curriculum and in physical education.

Measurement learned in mathematics, science and art can be explored in a concrete way through design and technology. Published mathematics schemes have included many apparent measurement activities which on analysis turn out to be no more than simple computation exercises. For example:

a. 4cm + 10cm = ☐cm
b. 2.3l + ☐l = 10l
c. kg   4.792
       2.641 −
       ─────

d. Find the perimeter of a rectangular lawn 10m by 12m.

Once children have acquired the relevant mathematical concepts and skills and have learned to use the appropriate measuring instruments and standard units, there is no longer a need to focus on measurement within the mathematics curriculum. The children now need to learn to apply their skills and knowledge and to develop further their understanding of measurement through the whole curriculum; in topic work, science, crafts, technology and so on.

Children need to build up a wide vocabulary of language associated with measurement. This helps them to describe and apply measurement to their activities.

The language of measurement can be divided into three categories: comparative, descriptive and technical.

Piaget stated that there are two fundamental operations of measurement – conservation and transitivity. It is therefore important that children are familiar with both before they can begin to measure.

• Conservation is the invariance of quantity, which is not dependent on any rearrangement. The amount of water remains the same

whichever way the bottle is tilted. A litre of cola is the same whether it is in a bottle with a one litre capacity or half filling a two litre bottle.

• Transitivity is a name given to the concept that if A = B and B = C, then A = C. It can be demonstrated by the use of a measuring instrument as a tool. The instrument can be standard, such as a ruler, or non-standard, such as a piece of string. For example, when measuring the width and depth of a window to make a new pair of curtains by using a tape

Comparative	Descriptive	Technical units	instrument
more	full	litre	measuring cylinder
same	empty		
heavier	heavy	metre	tape measure
weighs more	light		
longer	capacity	pound	coin
wide	weight		
today / tomorrow	time	degree	protractor
past / future	money		

measure, a grasp of transitivity allows us to be sure that the curtains will fit the window if they both have the same length according to the tape measure.

Indirect comparison using a measuring tool demonstrates the transitivity of measurement.

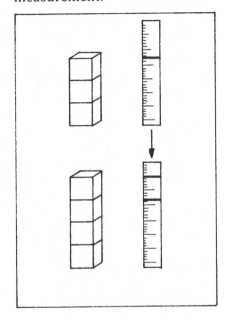

Attribute	Measurement	S.I.Unit
Distance	Length	Metre
Heaviness	Weight	Gram
Liquid	Capacity	Litre
Duration	Time	Second
Hotness	Temperature	°C celsius
Surface	Area	Area (100 sq metres)

The prolonged argument about the use of the terms 'mass' and 'weight' seems futile and therefore the term 'weight' has been used throughout, as it denotes heaviness and is the most familiar term to children.

Two other terms which cause some confusion are 'capacity' and 'volume'. Capacity is the concept of volume applied to liquids or materials which can be poured.

The main unit of capacity is the litre, which is divided into 1000 millilitres (equivalent to 1000 cubic centimetres). Volume is the amount of space occupied by a solid (external volume).

The main unit of volume is cubic metres (m³) or cubic centimetres (cm³).

The amount of space inside a container such as a box is called the internal volume or cubic capacity, and can be measured by using cubic units or litres.

Units of measurement are based on a consensus. They are all essentially arbitrary, as evidenced by the differing systems of measurement used throughout the world, such as imperial and metric. Children need to understand that the units they are taught are merely conventions designed to enable communication between people.

Money is often included as a form of measurement, and it has a number of similarities with other units. It helps us to describe the value of an object using an arbitrary unit, but it is a discrete scale and describes an abstract as opposed to a physical quantity. For example, the money scale is not infinitely divisible — 14.7p has no meaning in British currency. The notion of value cannot be directly and objectively measured. There is no '£3.99ness' about a paperback book, for example.

In this chapter we have provided some activities in which measurement can be used, but opportunities that are more relevant and fruitful will undoubtedly arise in your normal everyday curriculum. These should be exploited to the full.

ACTIVITIES

1. Shopping

Age range
Five to eight.
Group size
Pairs or small groups.
Objective
To compare and order objects by weight without measuring (conceptual development).
What you need
A variety of food packets, small bag of flour, shopping bag, balance.
What to do
Ask the children to put four packets into the shopping bag and to describe how it feels. They should then take out two packets and describe how the bag feels now. The children should pick up the packets one by one and compare them with the bag of flour. They can then sort them into three sets – those that are heavier than the flour, those that are lighter than the flour and those that feel about the same. Next they should check their sorting with a balance.

Further activity
Ask the children to use the balance to order the packets by weight. They should decide whether to order from the heaviest to the lightest or from the lightest to the heaviest and how they should undertake the task. They can also make some labels:

> Heavier
>
> or
>
> Lighter

and place them in the correct positions.

2. Profile of a favourite toy

Age range
Five to eight.
Group size
Individuals.
Objective
To use a range of measuring techniques to explore a stuffed toy (skills).
What you need
A range of standard and non-standard measuring instruments, children's favourite stuffed toys, photocopiable pages 154 to 155.

What to do
Over a period of time, allow the children to explore the measurements of their favourite toys. They should use either non-standard or standard units as appropriate, and record their results on pages 154 to 155.

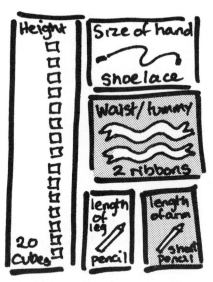

3. Multilink robots

Age range
Five to eight.
Group size
Pairs or small groups.
Objective
To weigh and order a range of objects (skills).
What you need
Multilink, balance and weights.
What to do
The children can make three different robots from Multilink. Then, using the balance to help them, they should put them into order according to weight. They should then make two

more robots and incorporate them into the order.

Next they can weigh each robot using the balance and weights, and record the results. They should also investigate the connection between the number of cubes in a robot and the robot's weight.

Further activity
See if the children can make a model robot from clay or dough that weighs the same as the middle Multilink robot in their order.

4. Cars in the garage

Age range
Five to eight.
Group size
Pairs or small groups.
Objective
To investigate area and volume through non-standard units (conceptual development).
What you need
An open-topped box, toy cars.
What to do
Ask the children to put the toy cars in the box. How many will fit if there is only one layer? Can they arrange them so that more cars can be fitted in?

BOX OF CARS

How many cars will fit in if two layers are allowed?

Further activity
Let the children repeat the activity, but this time using smaller toy cars. What do they notice? What happens if they use larger cars?

5. Money box

Age range
Five to eight.
Group size
Pairs or small groups.
Objective
To recognise and exchange coins up to £1 (skills).
What you need
Plastic or real coins, plastic tub for money box, counters, die, photocopiable pages 156 to 157.
What to do
The children take it in turns to throw the die and move their counters from the shaded start square. They take a coin of the same value as the square they land on from the money box in the centre of the board on page 156. Once the children have collected sufficient coins to exchange them for a single coin of a higher value, then they should do so. They should continue playing until someone has collected a 10p coin. The first player to do so is the winner, but the children may wish to continue playing until every player has finished the game.

The children can now repeat the game, but this time they should aim to collect a 20p piece. They can also use the board on page 157 to play the game, trying to collect first a 50p piece and later a £1 coin.

Further activity
The children can play the games again, but starting with an amount of money; 10p, 20p, 50p or £1. When the children land on a square showing a coin value, they must pay that amount into the bank. If they do not have a coin of the correct value then they should pay in a coin of a greater value and take out the right amount of change. The other players should check the transaction. They continue until one player has spent all of her coins.

6. Puddles

Age range
Five to eight.
Group size
Pairs or small groups.
Objective
To estimate and measure the area of a puddle at intervals through the day (conceptual development).
What you need
Puddle (real or made specially), chalk, squared paper, tape measure.
What to do
The children can draw round the edge of the puddle using a piece of chalk. They should do this at various intervals throughout the day. What do they notice?

See if the children can estimate the area of the puddle. They may find it easier to describe it in terms of cubes, bottle tops, tiles or other objects. They can then make a plan of the puddle and work out the area in square units.

7. Wet and dry

Age range
Seven to ten.
Group size
Pairs or small groups.
Objective
To investigate the weights of wet and dry objects (skills).
What you need
Items to measure (some that are absorbent, like a sponge, towel, paper towel, carpet tile or brick; and some that are not, like gravel, plastic, a paper-weight or plate), scales, tank of water.
What to do
First the children should weigh the dry objects and record the results. They then put each object in the water for a couple of minutes and weigh the objects again, while they are still wet. They should be able to calculate the difference between the wet and dry weights. Ask the children to weigh the objects after one hour. Can they explain what has happened?

Ask the children to make a table of the results so that it is clear to others what they have found.

	First		One hour later	
	Dry	Wet	Dry	Wet
Sponge				
Gravel				
Carpet				

8. How much will they hold?

Age range
Seven to ten.
Group size
Pairs or small groups.
Objective
To estimate the capacity of a range of containers (skills).
What you need
Four or five different plastic containers; for example, tomato trays, salad pots etc, labels, measuring jug, sand or water.
What to do
The children label each container with a letter. They can have a competition where each child puts the containers in order according to how much he thinks they will hold. Let the children test out their orders by filling each container with sand or water and measuring it in a calibrated jug.

9. Make a set of weights

Age range
Seven to ten.
Group size
Pairs or small groups.
Objective
To make a set of weights from modelling material, involving estimation and accurate measurement (skills).
What you need
Modelling material like Plasticine, flour, salt and water dough, self-hardening clay etc, set of weights, balance.
What to do
Ask the children to make a set of weights with modelling material. These can be checked by using the balance. The children can use their weights to weigh objects from the classroom.
Further activity
The children should research the history of weighing and weights. Can they discover how weights are made?

10. Time pictures

Age range
Seven to ten.
Group size
Individuals.
Objective
To use all of the bodily senses to gain a feeling of time (conceptual development).
What you need
A range of photographs from magazines, calendars etc, pencils, paper.
What to do
Ask the children to look at a picture and write about the time of day and of year which they think the picture shows. They should use clues to help them. What's the weather like? Is it daylight? Are there any shadows? Are there flowers? What are people wearing? What are people doing?

Holds less than ⓐ

ⓒ

Holds less than ⓑ

PLASTICINE

Further activity

Ask the children to go into the playground and close their eyes. They should try to use all their other senses to gain a feeling of the time of day and the season of year. What types of clues do they need to use to reach their conclusions? When you all return to the classroom, the children can write a time poem expressing their feelings and describing the clues they used outside.

11. Which units?

Age range
Seven to ten.
Group size
Pairs or small groups.
Objective
To decide which units are appropriate to various measurements (knowledge).
What you need
A selection of everyday objects.

Door height metre

Bottle capacity litre

Apple weight grams

Ribbon length feet

milk bottle capacity pint

Book length cm

What to do
The children choose three items each and decide which aspect of the items to measure – length, weight, volume and so on. They each tell a friend which objects they have chosen and then secretly decide which they think is the most appropriate unit of measurement to use, for example, centimetres, kilograms, litres etc. They can then ask their friend to guess which unit of measurement they have chosen.

12. Making cubes

Age range
Seven to ten.
Group size
Pairs or small groups.
Objective
To investigate volumes of cuboids by counting cubes (conceptual development).
What you need
Multilink.
What to do
Within each group, each child should make a different cuboid using Multilink. The groups should then investigate the sizes of the cuboids and the number of cubes needed to build them.

The children should keep together any cuboids that require the same number of cubes, and try to build other cuboids with that number of cubes.

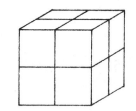

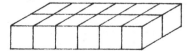

What relationship can they find between cuboids requiring the same number of cubes?

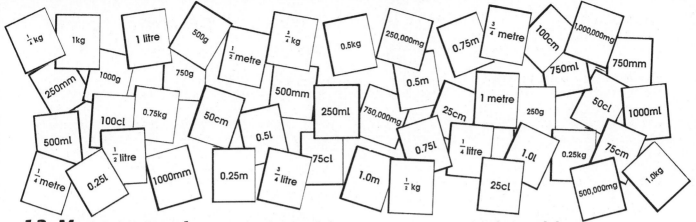

13. Measurement cards

Age range
Nine to thirteen.
Group size
Pairs or small groups.
Objective
To recognise equivalent measurements in decimal notation (skills).
What you need
Photocopiable pages 158 to 160.
What to do
Mount pages 158 to 160 on card and cut out along the black lines to make three sets of playing cards. The children then play a pairs or snap game with one of the sets. They can sort the cards into sets of four, and make some extra sets of four, for example:

$\frac{1}{5}$ metre	0.2m	20cm	200mm
$\frac{1}{8}$ kg	0.25kg	125g	125,000 mg
$\frac{3}{8}$ litre	0.375l	37.5cl	375ml

Further activity
The children can make up a game of their own to play with the cards.

14. Scale plan

Age range
Nine to thirteen.
Group size
Pairs or small groups.
Objective
To create an accurate scale plan (skills).
What you need
Rulers and tape measures, squared paper, drawing instruments.
What to do
Allow the children to choose a classroom wall display, and measure it as accurately as they can. Then they should create a careful scale plan of the display. Next they could investigate ways of rearranging the display to make it more effective.

Further activity
The children can design and plan a wall display using some of their own work. They should make it as eye-catching as possible, and ensure that the work will be displayed effectively. They can then mount and display the material.

Resources

Centicubes/Multilink
Rulers (30cm and metre)
Tape measures
Capacity measures
Balance and weights
Scales (personal, kitchen and spring balances)
Tank of water
Plastic containers
Packages and containers (some full)
Open-topped box
Shopping bag
Bag of flour
Children's favourite toys
Toy cars
Everyday items
Photographs from magazines
Modelling material
Coins
Counters
Dice
Chalk
Squared paper
Plain paper
Blank cards
Pencils.

CHAPTER 4

Shape and space

Children come to school with a multitude of experiences of the physical world, all of which are of a three-dimensional nature. These experiences are also almost exclusively sensory perceptions. The children see and make judgements related to fitting objects together and fitting themselves and other things into spaces; for example, pushing a trolley between two chairs, or packing a game away into a box and then putting the box into a cupboard.

Children do not separate their spatial awareness from their understanding of the properties of the objects around them. It is only in the classroom, because of the structure of the mathematics curriculum, that this somewhat unnatural division occurs.

BACKGROUND

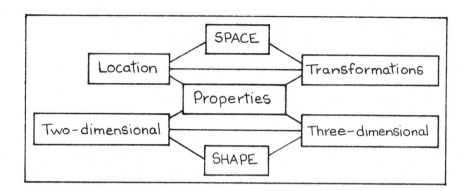

and mathematical concept. They cannot be represented by objects, because every object has three dimensions even if some are very small. The abstract nature of two-dimensional shapes is a frequent source of confusion to children, who often describe a door as a rectangle rather than a cuboid.

The concept of space encompasses both the position and the movement of objects in space. This is affected by the physical properties of the objects. Movements can be made in many directions – directions which correspond with the angles of shapes. Angles can therefore be used to describe the size of turn, as well as the properties of a shape or a direction. Reflection and rotation are both transformations; that is to say they are both movements. They can also be used to describe the symmetrical properties of shapes.

As children's early experiences of shape are of an exclusively

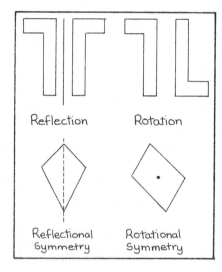

Reflection   Rotation

Reflectional Symmetry   Rotational Symmetry

three-dimensional nature, early work in school should be based on solid shapes to consolidate these valuable experiences. Two-dimensional shapes are purely an abstract

Children need to acquire a wide vocabulary and learn to apply it precisely to enable them to refine their perceptions and develop the concepts of shape and space. This vocabulary should include words that describe position in space, such as above, next to, beside; words that describe movements, such as straight, turning, reflecting; words that describe properties of shapes, such as sides, parallel, angles, congruent; and names of shapes, such as cylinder, isosceles triangle and trapezium.

ACTIVITIES

1. Shape jigsaw

Age range
Five to eight.
Group size
Pairs or small groups.
Objective
To recognise plane shapes and right-angled corners in shapes (knowledge).
What you need
Photocopiable page 161, scissors.
What to do
Look at the shape jigsaw on page 161 with the children. Ask them to cut along the dotted lines and point out the shapes which they have made. Ask them to look for a square, rectangle, triangle, pentagon and hexagon, and to sort out the shapes with right angles. How many are there?

The children can then put the shapes together to re-make the puzzle. Once the jigsaw is completed they can take a piece out and ask a friend to tell them what shape it is and whether it contains any right angles.

Further activity
Ask the children to choose a picture from a calendar or magazine. They should make three long cuts in it, at least two of which cross.

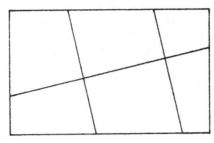

Together with the children, look at the shapes they have made. Are there any right angles? What would happen if they made one more cut? They can try it and see what happens.

2. Going home

Age range
Five to eight.
Group size
Pairs or small groups.
Objectives
To investigate routes on a 3×3 grid, and to give instructions for routes on a grid (conceptual development).
What you need
Photocopiable page 162, coloured pencils or pens.

What to do

Ask the children to investigate how many different routes the person can take on the way home, by going from dot to dot. The person cannot travel diagonally; only sideways, downwards and upwards. The children should work together in a group, and see how many different routes they can find.

They could then make a display of the routes they have found, collecting together examples of similar routes. Can they find any pattern in the number of routes of each type — for example, routes that start by going downwards and routes that start by going across?

Further activity

Ask the children to choose one route and describe it to a friend so that he or she can draw it on a spare grid. The children could also investigate routes on larger grids. Can they discover a pattern in their results?

3. PE

Age range
Five to eight.
Group size
Pairs or small groups.
Objective
To plan a PE game using apparatus (skills).
What you need
Two PE hoops, one chair, one rope, one bench, one mat.
What to do
In groups, the children should plan how the equipment will fit most effectively into the hall for a game.

They can make up a game using some or all of the equipment and describe how to play it, either writing or tape-recording the instructions. Then they can play the game.

4. Orienteering

Age range
Five to eight.
Group size
The whole class.
Objective
To use directional vocabulary and skills (skills).
What you need
Compass.
What to do
The children can set up a short orienteering course in the

school hall, playground or grounds. They should plan it carefully and compile instructions that include compass directions and distance. Distance can be described using non-standard or standard measures. At each point along the course there should be a word or picture to collect, and clear instructions for reaching the next point.

Ask the children to complete the course and describe their route using words such as turn, left, right, straight on, clockwise and anticlockwise. They should also refer to the points of the compass.

5. Feely box

Age range
Five to eight.
Group size
The whole class.
Objective
To investigate the properties of three-dimensional shapes (conceptual development).
What you need
A set of three-dimensional shapes, a 'feely' box or bag.
What to do
One of the children secretly places a shape in the box and asks the other children, in turn, to feel and describe it. One of the class should keep a note of the words used. The child should then change the shape for a similar one, but of a different size; for example a large and then a small cylinder. The rest of the children can then repeat the exercise using the feely box.

They can follow the exercise again using a different shape, although they should still keep varying the size of the shapes. Ask the children to compare the describing language they have used for the different shapes.

Further activity
Place an unusual item in the feely box, such as a piece of coral or jewellery, a clockwork toy, a pin cushion, some bubble wrap or a powder puff. Ask the children to describe what they feel and then draw what they think it looks like. When all the children have had a turn, they can compare their drawings with the real objects.

6. Junk models

Age range
Five to eight.
Group size
Pairs or small groups.
Objectives
To build with three-dimensional shapes and to use directional vocabulary (conceptual development).
What you need
A range of junk boxes, adhesive, baseboard.
What to do
Ask the children to build a model that fits in with a current topic, such as a farm, a town, a street, a railway station and so on. They can then give each other directions for moving an appropriate object such as a doll, car, horse, or train about the model.

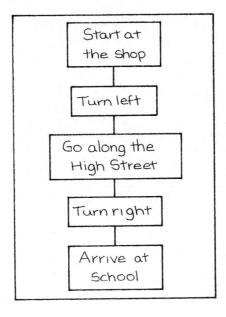

> Start at the shop
> Turn left
> Go along the High Street
> Turn right
> Arrive at School

The children can then make a flow chart to show the route they used.
Further activity
Ask the children to swap flow charts and to follow each other's routes around the model. Ask them to decide whether the instructions are clear or not.

7. Pin board

Age range
Seven to ten.
Group size
Individuals.
Objective
To investigate a 25-pin board (conceptual development).
What you need
A 25-pin board, elastic bands.
What to do
Ask the children to investigate different ways of using the elastic bands to divide the board into equal halves.

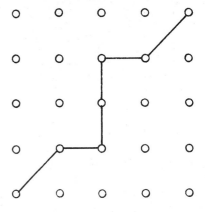

59

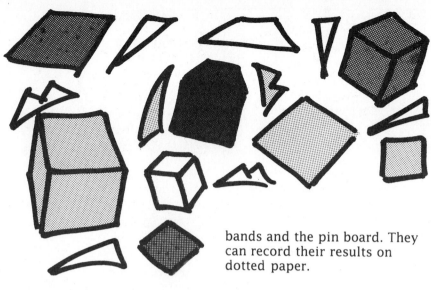

8. Turning shapes

Age range
Seven to ten.
Group size
Individuals.
Objective
To create shapes with rotational symmetry (conceptual development).
What you need
Squared paper with 2cm squares, Multilink.
What to do
Ask the children to make a flat pattern of five Multilink cubes. They should then place it on the squared paper and draw around it. Ask them to rotate it through 90° keeping one corner stationary. Once this is completed, they can draw the new shape.

They should repeat this two more times, creating a shape with rotational symmetry.

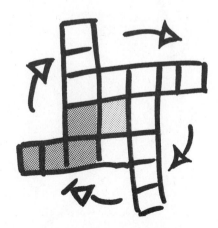

bands and the pin board. They can record their results on dotted paper.

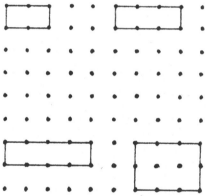

They should decide whether to include rectangles of the same size but in different positions, and whether they will include squares as rectangles.

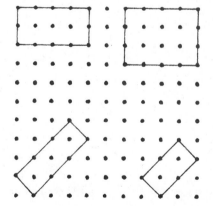

Next, ask them to try quarters. They should record their results on dotted paper.

How many different squares can they make on the boards? Ask them to investigate the areas and perimeters of the base squares.

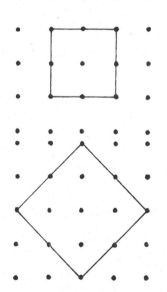

Further activity
Ask the children to investigate how many different rectangles they can make using elastic

Next, let the children make another pattern with five Multilink cubes and try to predict what shape it would make if rotated. They should try it and see what happens.

Further activity

The children can repeat the activity using a real object to rotate; for example, a key, a blunt knife, a pencil sharpener, an eraser or a coin such as a 50p or 20p piece.

9. Snails

Age range
Seven to ten.

Group size
Pairs or small groups.

Objectives
To describe position by using angle and distance and to investigate routes (skills).

What you need
Squared paper, pencils.

What to do
At a point where two lines cross on the squared paper the children should draw a line two squares long. Then they should turn 90° anticlockwise and draw a line three squares long, and then turn another 90° anticlockwise and draw a line one square long. They should keep going until a pattern forms.

This can be recorded using the symbols 90°, 2, 3, and 1.

Ask the children to try the activity again, keeping the angle the same but varying the order of the distances. What happens? Let them design some snail trails for themselves. Which trails are infinite, and which are repetitive?

Further activity
The children can alter the angle through which they turn to 45°, which allows for diagonal lines. Next, using isometric paper, they could form patterns which have angles of 60°.

The children can also try creating some trails incorporating four or five turns and different lengths of line.

10. Water lilies

Age range
Seven to ten.

Group size
Pairs or small groups.

Objective
To investigate reflective symmetry (conceptual development).

What you need
Photocopiable page 163, mirrors, counters.

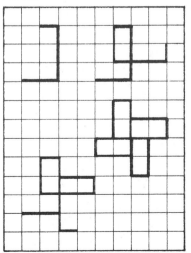

What to do
Using a mirror, each child chooses one of the arrangements of water lily leaves shown on the sheet. They should place the mirror in different positions and see what patterns they can make. Ask them to draw their favourite pattern. Then they can try with the other arrangements.

Let the children use two mirrors to see if they can make the leaves disappear. Can they double or treble the number of leaves? Which mirror angles can they use to double the number of leaves, to treble them and to make the leaves disappear?

Further activity
Ask the children to make an arrangement of their own, using counters. Let them use two mirrors to try to make different shapes. How can they make the counters form a square?

11. Nets

Age range
Seven to ten.
Group size
Individuals.
Objective
To make nets of three-dimensional shapes (skills).
What you need
Packages and boxes of varying shapes, such as cylinders, prisms, pyramids, cubes and cuboids, scissors, card, adhesive or sticky tape.
What to do
Each child chooses a container that is an interesting shape.

Making the minimum number of cuts in the container, they should lay it flat on the table and draw the net.

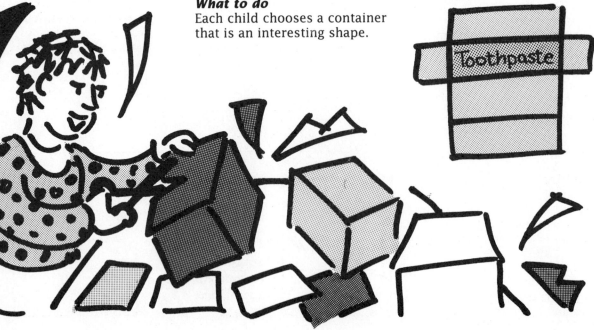

How many different nets can they make? They should then repeat this with containers of other shapes.

Further activity
Ask the children to design a net to make an interesting gift box. They can then make the box and decorate it attractively.

12. Straight cuts

Age range
Seven to ten.

Group size
Individuals.

Objective
To investigate making a range of two-dimensional shapes from a square (conceptual development).

What you need
Plain paper, drawing instruments, scissors.

What to do
Carefully, the children each draw a 15cm square on to the paper, making sure that the angles are 90°. They should then explore the range of shapes that can be made by drawing one line across the square. Ask them to make a list of the shapes they make.

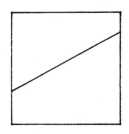

One line
triangle
trapezium
rectangle

Now they should use two lines that cross, and explore the shapes which can be made.

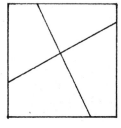

Two lines
triangle
Squares
rectangles
quadrilaterals

Further activity
Repeat the activity, but this time the children should start by drawing different shapes to divide, such as triangles, pentagons, and hexagons.

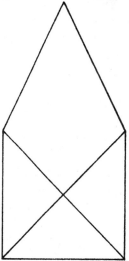

13. The supermarket

Age range
Nine to thirteen.
Group size
Pairs or small groups.
Objective
To investigate distances in networks (conceptual development).
What you need
Photocopiable page 164, ruler.
What to do
Ask the children to investigate the distances in the plan of the supermarket on page 164, using the scale of 1cm : 1m. They should try to work out the best route to follow in order to buy:

A pint of milk
Eggs
Cat food, cola
Ham
Jam
Bread
Frozen peas

The best route should be chosen by the children's criteria; it may be the shortest or the most efficient or logical – keeping similar goods together or buying eggs and frozen goods last.

Let the children investigate different routes around the shop to buy items of their own choice.

Further activity
Visit your local supermarket together and let the children make a plan. They can also explore different ways of displaying the goods, and report their ideas back to the supermarket manager.

14. Grids

Age range
Nine to thirteen.
Group size
Individuals.
Objective
To investigate traversable networks of grids (conceptual development).
What you need
Squared paper, pencils.

What to do
Ask the children to see if they can draw a 2 × 2 grid without lifting their pencils or going over the same line twice. Can they discover the largest number of squares in a 2 × 2 grid that they can draw in this way?

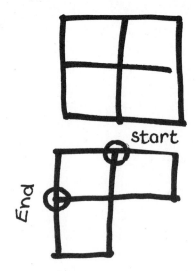

How many squares of a 3 × 3 grid can they draw?

15. The maze

Age range
Nine to thirteen.
Group size
Individuals.
Objective
To investigate routes through a maze (conceptual development).
What you need
Photocopiable page 165, pencils.

What to do
Ask the children to investigate routes around the maze, starting and finishing at the entrance, and visiting the centre at least once. Can they discover which is the shortest route, and which is the longest?

They should then investigate routes using the rule that they cannot walk down the same path twice.
Further activity
Let the children design their own mazes using a 14×14 grid. They can each ask a friend to investigate routes around the maze.

Ask them to try with a 4×4 grid. They can continue with other grid sizes. What happens if they use isometric paper?
Further activity
Let the children investigate shapes that can be drawn without lifting their pencils or going over the same line twice. They can invent their own and ask their friends to try to draw them.

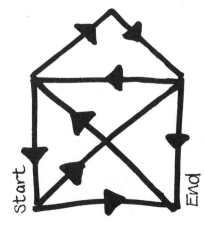

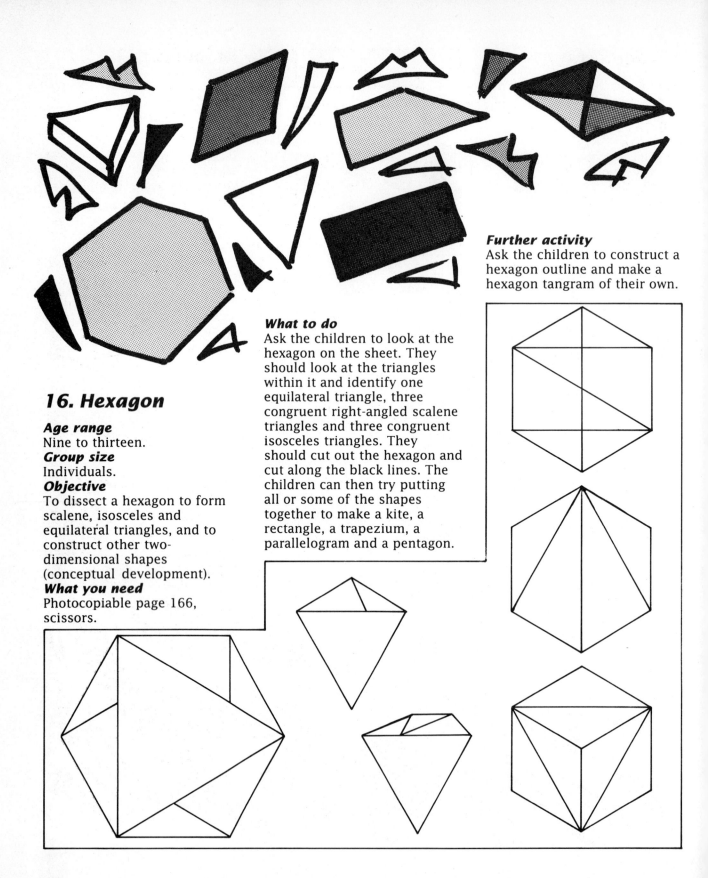

16. Hexagon

Age range
Nine to thirteen.
Group size
Individuals.
Objective
To dissect a hexagon to form scalene, isosceles and equilateral triangles, and to construct other two-dimensional shapes (conceptual development).
What you need
Photocopiable page 166, scissors.

What to do
Ask the children to look at the hexagon on the sheet. They should look at the triangles within it and identify one equilateral triangle, three congruent right-angled scalene triangles and three congruent isosceles triangles. They should cut out the hexagon and cut along the black lines. The children can then try putting all or some of the shapes together to make a kite, a rectangle, a trapezium, a parallelogram and a pentagon.

Further activity
Ask the children to construct a hexagon outline and make a hexagon tangram of their own.

17. Squares

Age range
Nine to thirteen.

Group size
Individuals.

Objective
To make squares from dissections of shapes (conceptual development).

What you need
Photocopiable page 167, scissors.

What to do
Together with the children, look at the shapes on page 167. Make one cut across the shapes so that the two pieces fit together to make a square.

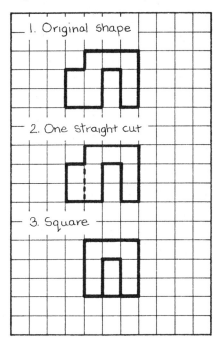

1. Original shape

2. One straight cut

3. Square

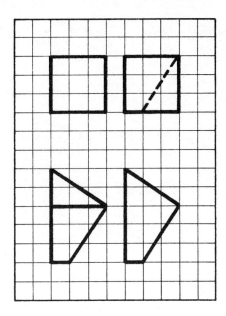

Further activity
Ask the children to draw a square lightly in pencil and mark a section on the square with a straight line. Next they should add the section on to the outside of the square, and draw firmly over the outline of the new shape. The children can then ask a friend to solve the puzzle – can they see how to make the shape back into a square?

Resources

Clixi
Polydron
Multilink
Mirrors
Pin boards
Squared paper
Isometric paper
Compasses (drawing and directional)
Scissors
Coloured pens
Pencils
PE equipment
Three-dimensional shapes
'Feely' box
Empty cardboard boxes and packages
Pin boards
Elastic bands
Counters
Rulers
Sticky tape
Adhesive.

CHAPTER 5

Data handling

Data handling covers four main aspects – collecting data, structuring data, looking for relationships and trends, and communicating the results. It incorporates a variety of statistical methods; for example, means and medians, probability theory and graphical representation.

Collecting data

Traditionally children have been given predetermined data to handle, which has not allowed them the opportunity to develop skills of data collection. It is essential that children have experience of collecting real data for a real purpose. It is more mathematically challenging and stimulating to discover, for example, sandwich preferences in order to plan the menu for the school party, than it is to draw a graph from given data in an exercise book.

The data collection methods are directly dependent on the reasons why the data are needed and the purpose for which they will be used. The collection methods need to be sensitive to the form of the data, and should not hinder the gathering of a full picture.

Children can develop their own methods of collecting data, and they should be encouraged to do so. However, there are a number of mathematical conventions which need to be taught directly. For example, children often find for themselves various methods of tallying, using ticks and so on, but the convention of grouping in fives for convenience and speed is something that should be taught.

Children's early attempts at data collection are often undertaken without prior planning. This tends to result in data being misplaced or lost, and in a subsequent lack of accuracy in the presentation of the data. The children should begin to develop methods of data collection that are more systematic and therefore verifiable. For example, young children often forget which people they have asked for data when collecting from a group. Gradually they realise the need to ask people in a logical order, or if this is not possible, to keep a record of who has been asked, using a class register or similar list of names. A more systematic approach to data collection should be encouraged and developed.

BACKGROUND

Data collection needs to be checkable as well as systematic. For example, there should be the same number of tally marks as people asked. Children should be encouraged to use checking methods throughout the data handling process.

It is also particularly important to bear in mind the purpose to which the data will be put and to identify any further information that may have a bearing on this. For example, it is likely that the time of day at which a car survey is held and the length of time for which it runs will be of relevance to the data collected. Other extraneous factors should also be noted – the weather for a car survey, the number of absentees for a class survey, the time of year for a wildlife survey.

Data collection can take many forms, including tally charts and questionnaires. It is beneficial for children to design these formats for themselves and to redesign them as necessary. There are a number of ways of keeping a tally:

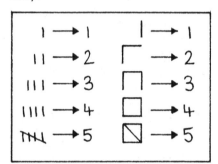

Mechanical and electronic aids can also be used; for example, clicking counters.

Alternatively you can set up a constant 'add one' function on a calculator:

Structuring data

It is important to structure the data before presenting it in graphical or other forms. It will need to be overviewed, and decisions will have to be taken

about how it should be ordered and structured. A simple computer database or graphics program can be very helpful when structuring collected data. Checks need to be made, however, on the accuracy of the data which is input, as it is easy to make mistakes at this stage which can materially affect the outcome.

Looking for relationships and trends

Data is collected and presented so that it can be interpreted, and in order that the information which has been gained can be acted upon. Interpretation involves looking for relationships and trends, both within a set of data and by comparing similar sets of data, which may have been collected over a period of time. An example of a relationship drawn from within a set of data is the observation that Cola is twice as popular as tea. A relationship drawn from similar sets of data over a period of time is the conclusion that there is more traffic on a Monday morning than any other weekday.

Older children should be given the experience of looking at published data, such as graphs in newspapers, to establish what relationships and trends are being communicated. They can also consider whether there is any information that is not being communicated and that would have been useful. For example, the chart below shows the popularity of certain car makes in some European countries, but does not communicate by how much certain makes are favoured, nor which other cars are sold in the countries, nor the total car sales in each country.

Country \ Preference	1st	2nd	3rd	4th
Great Britain	Ford	Vauxhall	Peugeot	Austin Rover
France	Renault	Peugeot	Citroen	Ford
Germany	Volkswagen	BMW	Mercedes	Ford
Spain	Seat	Ford	Nissan	Fiat
Italy	Fiat	Ford	Toyota	Opel
Greece	Ford	Fiat	Nissan	Toyota
Sweden	Volvo	Saab	Ford	BMW

Communicating results

In order to be able to communicate results meaningfully, we must conform to the graphical conventions. This means that we have to follow rules for creating graphs and rules for which type of graph is appropriate.

Why do we use graphs?
• To make comparisons.
• To present information and data visually, in a way that is more arresting, more meaningful, and more easily interpreted than a table of figures or words.
• To reveal the relationships that might otherwise pass unnoticed, or to highlight the equally important information that a relationship does not exist.
• To learn about the process of deciding what to do, which can be more important to understanding than the drawing of the graph.

When do we use graphs?
• They should be used throughout the whole curriculum.
• They should be developed out of a specific need.

Which graphs do we use?
Each type of graph can be used to display different types of information. From a topic such as 'Our class' a variety of data can be gathered.

• Arrow diagrams show a simple relationship. Only a small amount of data is required.

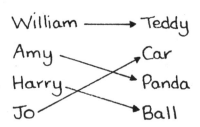

• Block graphs also show relationships between discrete

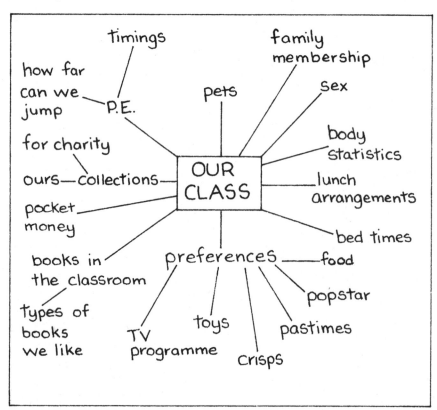

variables, but they do not allow the identification of individuals.

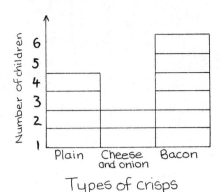

Types of crisps

• Set diagrams: there are two main ways of displaying the results of sorting according to two criteria – the Venn diagram and the Carroll diagram. From a set of items, four subsets are formed. Two criteria are required.

	Girl	~~Girl~~
School dinners	Jo	William
~~School dinners~~	Amy	Harry

Carroll diagram

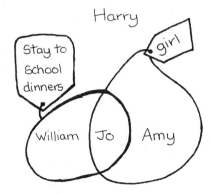

Venn diagram

• Bar charts handle continuous variables.

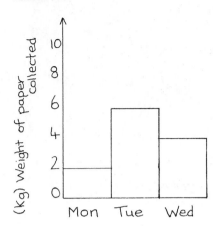

• Pictograms can be used to display large amounts of discrete information.

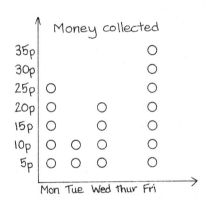

• Bar line graphs show the same type of information as bar charts.

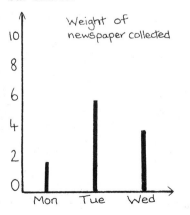

• Pie charts can be used to display the relationship between the parts of a whole.

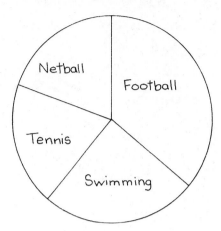

Our favourite sports

• Scatter diagrams are used to show the relationship between two variables.

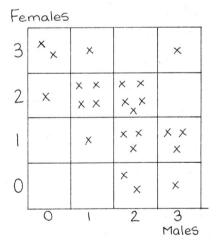

Our families

The activities included in this chapter are only examples from the wide range of available methods of data handling. Most of the activities focus on probability theory, as traditionally this has not been handled in the primary classroom.

ACTIVITIES

1. Sets from a box

Age range
Five to eight.
Group size
Pairs or small groups.
Objective
To identify a criteria for sorting and to apply it consistently (conceptual development).
What you need
A collection of interesting small objects for sorting, a box.
What to do
Put all the objects in the box and ask the children to choose three items each. They should then try to identify a common criterion between their own objects. If this is not possible, they can exchange their items for others in the box, but the chosen criterion should not be revealed. Then the children can choose a fourth item from the box that meets the secret criterion.

In their pairs, the children then try to identify their partner's criterion, and take it in turns to choose an item from the box which seems to meet it. If the first child guesses correctly, the children reverse roles. If the guess is wrong, the child whose criterion is being guessed may offer a clue to the other child such as the fact that it is something to do with shape.
Further activity
The children should record in their own way their partner's sets.

2. Towers

Age range
Five to eight.
Group size
Pairs or small groups.
Objective
To sort a number of sets and to record observations (conceptual developments).
What you need
Multilink cubes in three colours, large sheet of paper for recording.
What to do
Using only three colours, the children should make as many different towers of three cubes as possible.

They can then sort the towers into sets – those with three colours, those with two colours and those with one colour – and record their findings on the large sheets of paper.

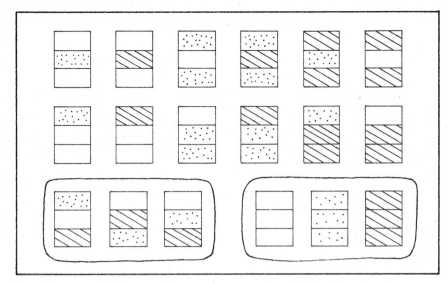

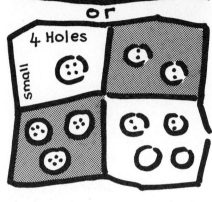

Further activity

Put coloured stickers on three chime bars. Ask the children to create a tune using the three notes.

3. Button jar

Age range
Five to eight.
Group size
Individuals.
Objectives
To sort objects and classify them by two criteria, and to record that sorting (conceptual development).
What you need
A button jar with an assortment of buttons, pencil, paper for recording.
What to do
Ask the children to sort some of the buttons according to one criterion, for example their colour, size, the number of holes, or what they are made of. The children should record this sorting.

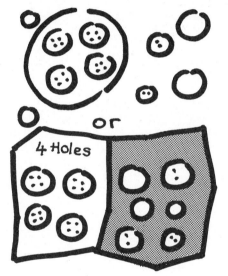

They can then choose another criterion and apply it to the sets, recording their sorting again.

Further activity

The children can play a 'Where does it come from?' game. One child secretly takes a button from the Venn diagram and shows it to her partner, who then has to describe where the button has come from and replace it. If the child places the button correctly he is given a point. The children continue playing, taking it in turns to guess, until one of them has gained five points.

4. Three-way sorting

Age range
Five to eight.
Group size
Pairs or small groups.
Objective
To use a Venn diagram for three criteria (skills).
What you need
Three-way Venn diagram on a large card, name cards.

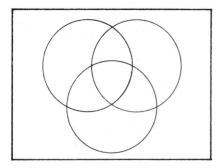

What to do
Choose three activities for the group to complete over a period of time; for example, you might set them the task of making a model, using the woodwork bench and using the computer.

As each child completes one of the activities on the list, ask him to move his name to the appropriate area of the Venn diagram.

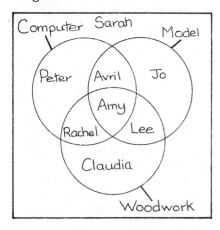

In this example, Amy has completed all three tasks, and Claudia has only done woodwork. Peter has only worked on the computer, while Rachel has done woodwork and worked on the computer.

5. Visitors to the school office

Age range
Five to eight.
Group size
Pairs or small groups.
Objectives
To keep a tally for a given period, and to complete a frequency table (skills).
What you need
Five-minute sand timer, clipboards.
What to do
Together with the children, discuss what time of the day might be the best to collect data about visitors to the school office. Ask the children to design a data collection sheet. For example:

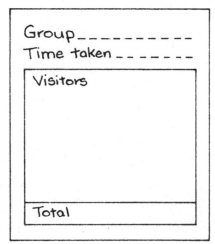

Discuss with the children how they could keep a record of the number of visitors to the school office. They may like to use either ticks or tally marks.

or

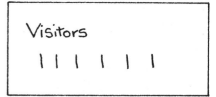

When the children have taken the tally for a while (say five, then ten, then fifteen minutes using the five-minute timer once, twice or three times) discuss with them ways of counting up the results.

The children may like to link sets of two tally marks or ticks.

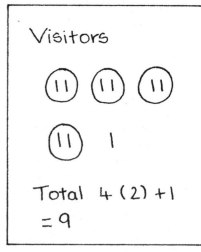

6. Is it possible?

Age range
Seven to ten.
Group size
Individuals.
Objective
To identify the likelihoods of different events (conceptual development).

What you need
Photocopiable page 168 to
make playing cards.
What to do
Mount photocopiable page 168
on to card and cut along the
black lines to make cards.

Girls are taller than boys.	All sides of an octagon are equal.	The number 6 is between 5 and 7.
A pint is more than a litre.	An hour is longer than a minute.	Two even numbers add up to an odd number.
Three 5p coins have a greater value than one 10p coin.	10 is half of 12.	May is before April.
There are 100g in a kilogram.	Days in summer are colder than days in winter.	A pentagon has 5 sides.

Ask the children to sort the
cards into three sets
depending on the likelihood of
their happening. They should
choose suitable words to
describe the sets, for example,
certain, always, definite, not
sure, maybe, possible,
impossible, never. Let the
children make up three more
statements of their own. They
can then ask a friend to add
them to the sets.

Further activity
Ask the children to make up
some statements for which
there is about an even chance
of them happening – for
example, that the result of
tossing a coin will be heads –
and ask them to add these to
the sets.

7. Timeline

Age range
Seven to ten.
Group size
Individuals.
Objective
To place events in order of
likelihood according to
whether there is more or less
than an even chance
(conceptual development).
What you need
Photocopiable page 169 to
make playing cards.
What to do
Mount photocopiable page 169
on to card and cut along the
black lines to make cards.

Tomorrow will be hot.	It will rain every day next week.
It will rain tomorrow.	It will snow on Sunday.
There will be a storm this month.	It will be dark by 9 o'clock tonight.
Tomorrow comes after today.	Tomorrow will be Sunday.

The children should try to sort
the cards into two sets – events
with a more than even chance
of occurring and events with a
less than even chance.
  They can then make up
some statements of their own
and add them to the sets.

8. Dice game

Age range
Seven to ten.
Group size
Pairs or small groups.
Objectives
To investigate the outcomes of
combined events and to collect
data (skills).

What you need
Photocopiable page 170, two
dice, counters.
What to do
Mount photocopiable page 170
on to card and cut along the
black lines to make cards. Ask
the children to lay out the digit
cards in a 3 × 3 grid from the
highest to lowest card.

3	4	5
6	7	8
9	10	11

  The children take it in turns
to throw the two dice. They
record the total and place their
counters on the appropriate
card. They must keep going
until one of them has covered
three cards in a straight line. If
they throw a total of two or
twelve, then they should have
another go. If they throw a
total that has already been
made, they should record it,
but they cannot place their
counter on the card.
  When the game is over the
children can examine the totals
they have thrown and choose
any three cards to remove.
They should re-form the grid
to make a 2 × 3 grid and play
the game again, still recording
the totals. Again, they should
choose three cards to remove.
They play again, placing the
cards in a line, and this time
note how many throws it takes
to cover the three cards.

Further activity
The children can calculate the
probability of throwing each
total of the two dice.

9. Marbles in a jar

Age range
Seven to ten.
Group size
Pairs or small groups.
Objective
To record the outcomes of events (conceptual development).
What you need
One yellow counter, two blue counters, three red counters, photocopiable page 171, bag.
What to do
Ask the children to place the counters in the bag. They should draw one counter out at a time, and record its colour by shading one marble in the jar the correct colour.

The counter is replaced each time, and the children continue picking out counters until the marbles are all coloured. What do they notice? They can now repeat the experiment with different numbers of each colour counter in the bag; for example, two yellow, four blue and five red.
Further activity
The children can choose the number of counters in the bag, so that one colour has very little chance of being picked, and then repeat the activity.

10. Phone calls to school

Age range
Seven to ten.
Group size
Pairs or small groups.
Objectives
To keep a tally over a given period of time, to complete a frequency table and to make comparisons between sets of data (skills).
What you need
Timer, clipboards.
What to do
Ask the children to organise themselves into a rota, so that they can count the number of phone calls made to the school at intervals throughout the day. They should also decide how long each group should keep the tally for; perhaps for ten minutes every hour.

The children should then design a data collection sheet to accommodate each group's data.

Time	Tally	Total
9 o'clock – 9.10	̶T̶H̶L̶ I	6
10 o'clock –10.10	I I I	3
11 o'clock –11.10	̶T̶H̶L̶ I I	7
12 o'clock –12.10	I I I I	4
1 o'clock –1.10	I	1
2 o'clock – 2.10	I I I	3
3 o'clock –3.10	̶T̶H̶L̶ ̶T̶H̶L̶	10

Discuss with the children the data they have collected. When was the busiest time for phone calls and when was the quietest? Why do they think this is?

Ask the children to repeat the activity on a different day of the week, and to compare the two sets of data. How are they similar and how are they different?

11. Dominoes

Age range
Nine to thirteen.
Group size
Pairs or small groups.
Objective
To use knowledge of probability to make predictions (skills).
What you need
A set of dominoes.
What to do
The children should lay out the set of dominoes face downwards on the table. They can then turn over a domino and record the total number of spots. They should do this several times.

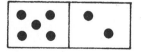

They should then investigate the totals of all the dominoes. Which number are they most likely to turn up? What is the probability of this?

Let them investigate how many dominoes they have to turn over in order to get the most likely total. When they try again, is the result the same?

12. Dice pie chart

Age range
Nine to thirteen.
Group size
Individuals.
Objectives
To keep a tally of dice throws and to construct a pie chart (conceptual development; skills).
What you need
Die, protractor, compasses.
What to do
Ask the children to throw the die 36 times and keep a tally of the result of each throw.

Throw	Tally	Total
1	IIII	4
2	THL I	6
3	THL III	8
4	THL	5
5	THL IIII	9
6	THL	4

They should then construct a pie chart to show their results, using an angle of 10° to represent each throw.

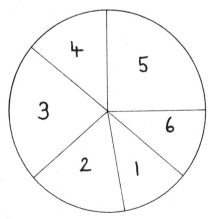

The children can compare their pie charts. Can they work out the probability of throwing a six?

13. Shopping times

Age range
Nine to thirteen.
Group size
Pairs or small groups.
Objective
To collect data to show patterns of shopping and to report findings (skills).
What you need
Timer, clipboards.
What to do
Ask the children to plan how they can keep a tally of shoppers visiting a local store during one day. They should take it in turns to collect the data, preferably in pairs.

Before they go out they should design a group data collection sheet.

Time	Male		Female		Total
9.01 –10.00	III	3	THL I	6	9
10.01 – 11.00	IIII	4	THL II	7	11
11.01 –12.00	THL	5	III	3	8
12.01 –13.00	THL II	7	THL THL	10	17
13.01 –14.00	II	2	IIII	4	6
14.01 –15.00	I	1	THL III	8	9

When the results have been collected, discuss them with the children. Suppose every shopper spent £1.00 in the shop, how much would the shop have taken? What about £5.00? What about £10.00? Were there more male or female shoppers? Why do they think this might be? Which time of day was the busiest and which the quietest? Why do they think this happens? Do they think it will always be the same?

Ask the children to prepare a report of their findings and conclusions to present to the shopkeeper or manager. The report should include written statements, graphical representation and tables and charts. It should communicate clearly what the children have found. The children may like to use a comparative bar chart.

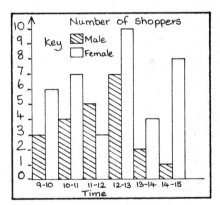

Resources

Various sizes of squared paper
Dice
Dominoes
Counters
Bag/box
Multilink.

CHAPTER 6

Mathematics in the whole curriculum

This chapter will examine mathematics in a wider context both across and throughout the whole primary curriculum, with strategies for planning cross-curricular work and ideas for developing real problem-solving skills.

The first three sections focus on different approaches to integrating mathematics with other subjects. The fourth section describes a method of planning and organising a cross-curricular project. The final section suggests ways of stimulating the children's mathematical thinking and promoting discussion.

1. Mathematics as the focus for the curriculum

Mathematics is often seen as the servant of the rest of the curriculum, but this need not always be the case. Often mathematics can be the starting point for other areas of study. For example, the study of number can include research into the development of numbers and mathematical symbols through the ages and across the world. A study of the Fibonacci series could involve investigating its relevance to nature and to architecture.

The following diagrams relate to different areas of mathematics. The text boxes contain ideas for activities in different curriculum areas, and each activity has been given a number from one to three depending on its level of difficulty. Each mathematical area is used as a starting point for other areas of learning and experience. The ideas are not exhaustive, and not all areas of learning and experience are covered; the diagrams are meant as starting points for planning and for extension to other areas.

Human and social
2. Ask the children to investigate how and why numbers are used around them, for example in house numbers, prices and road signs. They should classify their findings.
3. With the children, look in magazines and newspapers for percentages. What do they represent? Whom do they affect?

Linguistic and literary
1. Ask the children to listen to a few number rhymes and see whether they can remember their favourite.
3. Two children carefully describe a task. They work together to produce a flow chart detailing the task so that another person could follow it.

Language
2. The children could research the words used in other languages for numbers.

Number

Physical
1. In PE, divide the children into groups of two, three, and so on. Each child in the group is given a number, and they then respond to instructions according to their number.

Scientific and technological
1. Ask the children to make a pictorial flow chart to show the stages of planting a bulb or seeds. Label the stages first, second, third etc.
2. Ask the children to weigh out 400g of dry sand, and add three tablespoons (45ml) of water to it. They can read the new weight from the scales and continue adding water until the sand is very wet. They should keep a table of their results.
3. Investigate pulse rates by asking the children to take their pulse before exercise. They should then take it again immediately after exercise and at five minute intervals until it returns to the original rate.

Aesthetic and creative
1. Collect together some number symbols from magazines, newspapers etc. Ask the children to sort them into separate groups and make a collage of each symbol.
2. The children should draw several 5cm squares and find various ways of drawing one line that cuts them in half. They can then paint the halves. The children can try using two lines to make quarter squares.
3. The children should choose a recipe, and double the quantities so that it will feed twice as many people. Then they can work out the necessary quantities of ingredients for the number of people in their class.

Physical
2. Ask the children to design symbols to represent running, hopping, walking and turning. They can then hold up different symbols and ask their friends to move in that way.

Scientific and technological
1. Ask the children to look at a weather map and find out what some of the symbols represent. They can try to design some clear symbols of their own.
2. Investigate patterns in nature, for example those found in fir cones, shells, honeycombs and leaves.
3. Together investigate the use of symbols in science, including electrical and chemical symbols.

Aesthetic and creative
1. Ask the children to design their own printing blocks from clay or a similar type of material and make a printed pattern using three colours.
2. Ask the children to design some instructional/warning signs for the school, without using words.
3. Ask the children to start a pattern with Multilink using square, triangular or Fibonacci numbers. They can increase the pattern using a variety of colours.

Algebra

Linguistic and literary
1. Ask the children to make up tunes using chime bars. Ask them to change the rhythm. They should colour code each chime bar and record their tunes.
2. The children could write poems with strong rhythms and recite them while clapping to the rhythm.
3. The children should make a pattern from Multilink, and then hide it. Can they describe it to a friend so that he or she can make the same pattern?

Human and social
1. Ask the children to look at patterns of house numbers. Are all roads numbered in the same way? Are there any missing numbers? How are blocks of flats numbered?
3. The children can investigate historical population figures, including birth and death rates in the locality.

Physical
1. Choose four linked movements and ask the children to do them first very slowly, and then slightly quicker. They can then repeat the movements very quickly indeed.

Scientific and technological
1. Together with the children, plant a seed and measure the seedling as it grows. The children can record their findings.
2. Ask the children to test the bounce of three different types of ball, measuring how high the balls can bounce.
3. Ask the children to design an experiment to test various materials for strength or other properties.

Aesthetic and creative
1. The children should wrap up some parcels, and decorate them attractively. They can then describe them to a friend.
2. Using a ruler, pencil and compass the children should try to design a picture.
3. The children could enlarge a photograph or picture using a grid and then compare it with the original.

Measurement

Linguistic and literary
1. Ask the children to draw a picture and write a sentence about what happened yesterday, what is happening today and what they hope will happen tomorrow.
2. Ask the children to plan a journey for a day's outing, using timetables and price lists. They should also write an advertisement for this day trip.
3. Ask the children to write a story about a journey in which they include measurement details such as time, distance, cost, speed, temperature and so on.

Human and social
2. The children can investigate differences between people of different ages, for example, in terms of height, weight, bed-times, how much food they eat, and so on.
3. Ask the children to investigate the differences between metric and imperial measures and to discover which units people prefer to use.

Physical
2. The children can devise and play a game that uses compass drections and 'clockwise' and 'anti-clockwise'.

Scientific and technological
1. Ask the children to build a model house from junk. They should make it as detailed as possible, and include some internal items.
2. The children should investigate the strengths of various shapes and build a tower or a bridge using strong shapes.
3. Together with the children investigate shapes in architecture including bridges, towers and churches.

Aesthetic and creative
1. Ask the children to create a picture that shows objects under, next to and behind other items.
2. Ask the children to create patterns by rotating shapes.
3. Ask the children to design and create a treasure map. They should try to make it look old and battered. They should also include written instructions for finding the treasure.

Shape

Linguistic and literary
1. Act out a story such as *Bears in the Night*, Stan and Jan Berenstain (Collins), *Rosie's Walk*, Pat Hutchins (Bodley Head).
2. Ask the children to choose a shape and make up a story that includes the shape as often as possible. They can also draw a picture to illustrate their story.
3. Ask the children to describe carefully a circular route round the school, taking note of landmarks and points of interest.

Human and social
1. With the children, look around the school for shapes which fit together. Let the children take some rubbings, and ask them to label them to show where they came from.
3. The children could explore the symmetry of patterns from different cultures.

Aesthetic and creative

1. Together, take a survey of favourite colours. The children can use the most popular colours to paint or embroider a picture.

2. Ask the children to design a board game using spinners, dice or cards.

3. Ask the children to make up a game of chance and decide on the criteria for winning and the allocation of points. For example, they might like to design a 'roll a penny' game.

Scientific and technological

1. Go with the children on a walk to collect a variety of leaves. The children should sort the leaves and explain their criteria.

2. Ask the children to design a decision tree which they can use to sort a few leaves or twigs. They can then ask a friend to try it out.

3. Ask the children to keep weather records and present them graphically.

Data handling

Human and social

1. Together with the children, take a survey of how the children in the class come to school.

2. Together, take a class survey of pocket money. The children can draw a graph and calculate the mean and the range of the data. Ask them to compare their findings with another class.

3. Ask the children to look at some television viewing figures. They should make graphs, look for trends, and try to explain variations in these. They can also take a survey of their friends and compare it with the national figures.

Linguistic and literary

1. Ask the children to collect together words which describe the relation between sets of two or three pictures.

2. Ask the children to write a story which involves the reader in choosing different routes and alternative endings.

3. Ask the children to design a questionnaire to take a survey of people's preferences in respect of television programmes, food, sport, books, colours and so on.

2. Mathematics from other areas of the curriculum

The following diagrams are examples of a more common approach to planning cross-curricular projects, in that specific topics have been chosen – 'Our school and us' and 'Celebrations' – and the mathematical possibilities explored.

The topics have been separated into three levels of difficulty, and the suggestions given here are by no means exhaustive. They are intended purely as examples of the way topics can include a range of mathematics as well as the more usual cross-curricular areas of learning such as geography, history and language. Mathematics is rarely included in cross-curricular topics although there are plenty of opportunities to develop mathematics beyond what is traditionally taught. Cross-curricular topics allow children to use and apply their mathematical learning and skills.

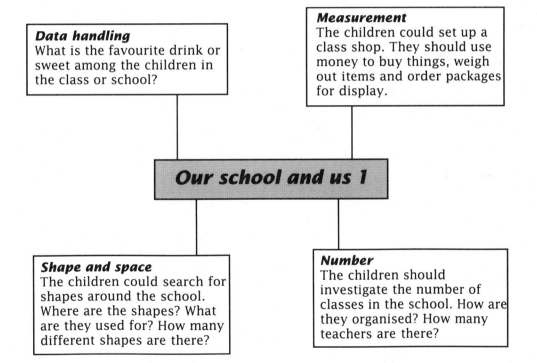

Data handling
What is the favourite drink or sweet among the children in the class or school?

Measurement
The children could set up a class shop. They should use money to buy things, weigh out items and order packages for display.

Our school and us 1

Shape and space
The children could search for shapes around the school. Where are the shapes? What are they used for? How many different shapes are there?

Number
The children should investigate the number of classes in the school. How are they organised? How many teachers are there?

Data handling
The children could organise a class party. They should find out which are the most popular foods and games, and work out which ingredients will have to be bought and in what quantities. They should also consider what sorts of prizes will have to be bought and what would be the most popular sort of music.

Shape and space
The children could make a plan of the classroom, and make a scale model. They could find the school on a local map.

Our school and us 2

Measurement
The children could buy some ingredients and make some cakes and snacks for the class party. They should increase the quantities in the recipes in order to make enough for everyone.

Number
The children can investigate the number of pupils in the school. How many boys and how many girls are there? How many children have school dinners, packed lunches or go home to lunch? How many children are there in each class?

Number
Ask the children to investigate how many pencils will need to be bought so that there will be enough to last the school for one year.

Data handling
The children could take a survey of opinions about school dinners and the meal and break-time arrangements. How can these things reasonably be improved?

Our school and us 3

Measurement
The children can investigate how far they travel to school and how long it takes them. Does the person who lives nearest take the shortest amount of time to get to school?

Shape and space
The children should plan and set up a short orienteering course in the school grounds. They can ask friends to try it out.

Measurement
The children can plan the timetable for the event. How long will it last? Will everyone arrive at the same time? When will the snacks be served?

Shape and space
The children can make a plan of the floor space to be used for the celebration, constructing models of any required features. Where should the ticket seller be positioned? Where should the music be? Is there enough space for all the people who will be attending?

Number
The children can investigate the number of children, parents and friends attending the celebration. How many children? How many adults? How many teachers? How many children from each of the classes?

Celebrations 1

Data handling
The children could find out what are the favourite party games. What snacks would everybody like? Do adults and children have different preferences?

Measurement
The children can organise a 'float' of money for the celebration. They can be the accountants, arranging for bills to be paid and accounting for any expenses incurred by children or staff.

Shape and space
Ask the children to work out how many chairs will be needed, and to plan the location and the best arrangement for them. They can organise a list of classes which will be providing chairs, and work out routes the people providing the chairs can follow.

Number
The children can use the school records to find out how many people have attended previous celebrations. They can compare these attendance figures with the data collected by the younger children.

Celebrations 2

Data handling
The children can research the most popular music for the celebration. Does everybody like the same type of music? They can make a list of people who can provide the records or tapes which have been chosen.

Number
The oldest children could cost out the celebration and work out how much tickets should cost. They could also buy the snacks and drinks, basing their purchases on the number of tickets sold or the number of people who have said they would attend.

Shape and space
The children could draw up scale plans of the school premises which will be used for the event. Salient features such as the canteen, cloakrooms etc could be added. They could also design a logo for use on programmes, decorations, furniture etc.

Children who are involved in the detailed planning of a community event should be encouraged to make a report of their findings and present them to the governors, school fund organisers and local community representatives.

Celebrations 3

Measurement
Ask the children to plan a timetable for the event, and make a compilation audio-cassette containing several pieces of music lasting a specified time.

They can set up a soft drinks bar and decide how many bottles of different types of drink to buy. How many glasses can be obtained from one bottle? How much should be charged for each drink in order to make a small profit for charity?

Data handling
Games and activities will vary according to the age groups attending. The children could survey the age range expected and look for age-related trends in music, snacks and games.

Real problem solving

The likelihood is that you and the children will be continually involved in solving real problems. These situations have not been set up deliberately by you, but have arisen naturally from the children's questions and concerns.

These problems present themselves naturally during everyday school life; for example, an untidy cloakroom to clear up, rotas to organise or a class display to plan. All of these activities can be approached and handled by the children themselves, and all have a real purpose. They will all necessarily include a great deal of mathematical thinking.

In *Mathematics Counts* the Cockcroft Committee argue that 'All children need experience of applying the mathematics they are learning both to familiar everyday situations and also to the solutions of problems which are not exact repetitions of exercises which have already been practised' (Para 321, 1982).

Inevitably problem solving is cross-curricular, but many mathematical concepts, skills, strategies and attitudes are central to reaching a sensible solution.

If we are to capitalise on the problems that arise unexpectedly in the classroom, we have to be prepared to be flexible and put aside our planning programme. This should not worry us, as it is only the use of mathematics for solving problems that gives it any real meaning or place in the curriculum.

Problem solving can be broken down into seven main stages:

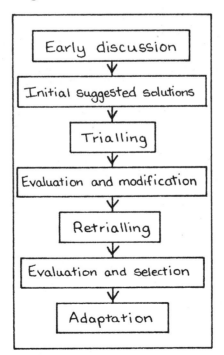

Early discussion
↓
Initial suggested solutions
↓
Trialling
↓
Evaluation and modification
↓
Retrialling
↓
Evaluation and selection
↓
Adaptation

Throughout the problem solving exercise the children will need to use a variety of strategies. Observation, classification, brainstorming and reflection predominate in the early stages. The children need to be logical about their approach, and they also need to bear in mind the constraints of the real situation and remember that the 'ideal' solution may not always be viable.

Later stages of the process involve strategies such as hypothesising, questioning, data collection, trial and error, reasoning and trialling. The children will also need to create a method of recording their information and presenting it to an audience – you, their friends or another person who can make judgements and decisions; for example, the headteacher.

It is important that the solution is not purely hypothetical and that it can actually be carried out. It is also important that throughout the process the teacher has taken a back seat and has allowed the children to determine their own approaches to the problem so that they can become independent learners. The teacher's role, therefore, becomes that of a facilitator rather than that of a leader.

A real problem
Context
The school was unable to have the usual teacher-organised sports day, and the children were disappointed. So two classes of six- to seven-year-olds worked together to organise their own event. Sometimes all 60 children worked together, and at other times the classes worked separately.

Processes
• Initially both classes came together to brainstorm and the children identified 20 points that would have to be considered; for example, what date could they hold the sports day on, how many drinks would they need, how would they mark the track and so on.
• A list of tasks was drawn up and prioritised; for example, the headteacher's permission was asked first, but putting out the chairs was left to the morning of the event.

• Most important was the enthusiasm of the children, which seemed to be generated because the event was their own. They soon recognised the need to plan in a logical way. The children also came to understand the constraints that can affect planning, often leading to the need to review and alter their procedures. A great sense of fairness was evident, as was the recognition of the need to work together for the good of the whole group.

Mathematics involved
• Number: addition (for example, of the total number of children involved); subtraction (in making sure that everybody was involved in at least one event); multiplication (in calculating the number of people required for the team events); sharing (when planning refreshments); estimation (for example, of the number of chairs needed for the spectators).
• Algebra: ordering (when planning the order of the events); sequencing (when laying out the track for an obstacle race).

• Measurement: of time (when timing the length of the races); of money (when costing the refreshments); of length (when measuring the race courses); of volume (when packing away the equipment); of capacity (when making the refreshments).
• Data handling: collecting information (about who wanted to be in which event); recording (the results of events); presenting data (reporting the results); interpreting data (analysing results by classes.

The processes of solving mathematical problems were evident throughout, including raising and answering questions, recording, checking results, selecting the materials and the mathematics to use, talking about the work, and adopting a systematic approach.

4. Planning a cross-curricular theme

There are many opportunities for developing mathematics across the whole primary curriculum, whether mathematics is the starting point for a topic or whether it is developed through an idea from another area of learning and experience. Mathematics is a process, an action that people use to organise, represent and communicate information. Whenever people classify and organise information into logical frameworks they are acting mathematically. It is not only actions in which numbers are used that may be called mathematical.

The curriculum that children experience in school can be classified into three closely interrelated aspects: the areas of learning and experience; the elements of learning, and the teaching approaches. These aspects cannot be easily separated, but it is necessary to identify some factors that make each aspect distinct in order to plan the curriculum in an organised way.

The areas of learning and experience
Curriculum content is usually organised either as subjects or as areas of learning and experience. When planning a cross-curricular theme it helps to see the curriculum as areas of learning and experience rather than as discrete subject areas. *Curriculum 5 to 16* lists nine areas of learning and experience: aesthetic and creative, human and social, linguistic and literary, mathematical, moral, physical, scientific, spiritual and technological.

The elements of learning
There are five main elements of learning identified in *Curriculum 5 to l6*: facts, concepts, skills, strategies and attitudes.

• Facts are pieces of information which may be isolated, like knowledge of the names of shapes.
• Concepts are ideas that are fluid and interconnected. They grow and change as we develop. A child's concept of 'subtraction' or 'four' will change as more experiences are encountered.
• Skills are methods of completing a task either physically or mentally, and apply to activities like drawing a circle or using a calculator.
• Strategies are ways of solving problems; what to do and how to do it. For example, trial and error, looking for patterns and hypothesising are strategies.
• Attitudes are the emotions we bring to a task. They affect how we tackle a task, and even whether we approach it at all.

It is important that children are given the opportunity to develop in all the five elements of learning, and that a cross-curricular theme allows all the elements to be incorporated and used together.

The teaching approaches
The Cockcroft Report identified six main teaching approaches for mathematics: exposition, discussion, practical work, practice and consolidation, investigative work and problem solving. All these approaches have a part to play, and different activities require different approaches. Often more than one approach is adopted within an activity.

These three aspects of the curriculum are closely interrelated and affect one another.

It is important to highlight the main reasons for adopting a cross-curricular approach as opposed to a subject-based approach. People do not experience the world in different categories, and solutions to the problems encountered rarely fit neatly into subject boundaries. Cross-curricular work provides children with an overall view of the curriculum, and thereby encourages the transfer of knowledge between subject areas. Many concepts have a basis in several subjects and can only be properly developed by a child if she can see the connection and draw the various aspects of experience together. This also applies to strategies such as hypothesising, which has a basis in many areas, including mathematics, science and technology; and to skills such as measuring, which has a basis in most areas of learning and experience. The cross-curricular approach can also encourage positive attitudes in children, and it presents the curriculum as relevant and purposeful.

It is necessary to ensure when planning a theme that, over a period of time, a broad, balanced curriculum is offered to the children. It is also necessary to devise a programme that ensures a progression of the elements of learning. If the children are to learn and develop they need to be stimulated with new and challenging experiences.

Many cross-curricular topics have their foundation in one area of learning and experience, but will range more widely when developed. Many topics or themes will involve six or seven areas of learning and experience, but very few will involve all nine. It is important not to force connections, as this presents the children with a fragmented and mysterious curriculum.

The planning grid

The grid below is designed to be an aid in the initial stages of planning a cross-curricular theme. It has room to include eight areas of learning and experience. As an aid to future planning and to ensure a broad and balanced curriculum over the year, we have listed all the nine areas of learning and experience and suggest that these could be ticked, underlined or highlighted to help identify the areas not covered in any particular theme.

The first box identifies the fundamental area of learning and experience for this topic. This particular topic has a scientific basis but any of the nine areas of learning and experience could provide a starting point for a stimulating cross-curricular theme.

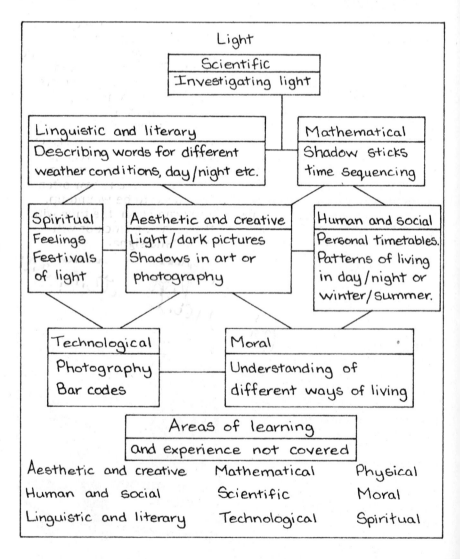

5. Stimulating mathematical thinking and discussion

Interest areas

One common method of stimulating children into thinking and questioning is to set up an interest area in the classroom. However, it seems to be quite unusual to set up an area with a mathematical focus. An area with a mathematical theme will help to promote the children's curiosity about mathematics. It can also be used to stimulate the children's interest in a new topic within mathematics. An interest area could include some short activities that extend the children's mathematical experience and that can be done in spare moments. This will help children to recognise that mathematics can be fun and that it is based in the real world. The following are examples of items that can be included on an interest table, together with ideas for developing mathematics.

Collections

• Clocks: the children can compare the faces of various clocks. What type of numerals do they have? Different types of clock can be compared, for example, digital, water, pendulum, marble, candle, and so on. The children could investigate clocks which are used for different things, for example alarm clocks, timers, car clocks, watches, cuckoo clocks, grandfather clocks etc. The children can investigate whether the clocks keep good time and find out how often they need to be wound up. They can check the time with the speaking clock or with radio time signals.

Grandfather clock
Alarm clock
watch

• Containers: the children can investigate the way a similar design is used for containers of different sizes by looking at a variety of boxes from one range of perfume or toiletries, or comparing different sized chocolate boxes.

perfume
talc
perfume
soap

• Measuring instruments: a range of these can be displayed, so that the children can think about what the different instruments are for and how they are used. A display can then be made with the instruments labelled by name and by purpose, with instructions explaining how they should be used.

• Graphs from newspapers: these can be collected and displayed so that children can discuss what the graphs tell the readers, and also what they do not tell. Do the children think that the graphs represent the information fairly, or have tricks been used to distort the data?

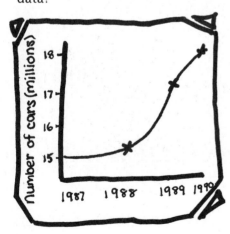

• Ceramic tiles: these can be used to explore tessellation, symmetry, fractions etc. They are also a possible source of inspiration for aesthetic designs.

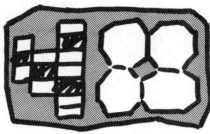

• Wheels and gears: these can be a starting point for investigations of diameter, radius and circumference and ratio.

• Calendars: these can be used to explore number patterns and relationships, to decide whether a certain year was a leap year, to find out the number of Mondays in one year and to investigate the length of school terms. They can also form the basis for many other activities.

A square of numbers can be chosen from a month's calendar, and the totals of the rows, columns and diagonals can be investigated.

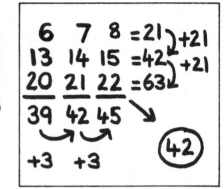

Estimation activities
• The number of items in a jar.
• The weight of a cake.
• The capacity of various containers.
• The length of a ribbon.
• The time needed to perform a task.
• Objects which weigh the same.

These estimation activities can be set up and left for the children to explore and comment upon before a discussion and ordering of the actual results. Were the estimates close to the real measurement or count?

The senses

Developing the senses individually will stimulate different types of mathematical language. The following lists explore one item in detail and list other starting points.

• Things to see: fabrics, periscope, kaleidoscope, photographs from odd angles, postcards of famous paintings, magnification, mirrors, prisms.

These should be used to stimulate mathematical discussion through observation. They can also be used to begin a mathematical topic. For example, a kaleidoscope can stimulate ideas of symmetry, reflection and fractions.

drum beats, a metronome, waves and a dripping tape can be used to explore rhythms and beats.

• Things to hear: tape-recorded sounds, music shakers with different fillings, chime bars hit with different beaters, small and large pebbles, different papers to be scrunched, stretched elastic bands, jars with different levels of water.

A tape-recorded collection of sounds like heart beats, clocks,

• Things to touch: fabrics, mechanical items, alarm systems, battery operated games, magnets, textures, Newton's cradle, a gyroscope. These should be used to stimulate an exploration of how things work and the mathematics behind the object. For example, would Newton's cradle work if all the strings suspending the balls were of different lengths, or all the balls were different sizes?

• Things to smell: spices, herbs, flowers, fruit.

This can stimulate discussion about where these things come from. What part of the plant are they from? Which plants are used for perfumes? Comparisons can be made between the flowers and the perfumes – compare lavender and lavender water, for example.

• Things to taste: food, flavourings, range of edible white powders, drinks.

Guessing games can be played and lists made of who guessed which flavour correctly. Surveys can be taken to see which is the most popular flavour. Can the children tell margarine from butter? Is it harder with their eyes closed? Ask them to test the different varieties of cola. Which strawberry yoghurt tastes most like strawberries?

Stories

All classrooms contain a selection of story books. These can be a fruitful source of ideas for mathematical investigation. It is important to keep the ideas as close to the story as possible; otherwise the children can easily lose the connection.

Popular stories are a rich source of ideas for introducing young children to the enquiry-based approach to learning mathematics. The most fruitful activities are those which arise from stories that focus on events that the children may have encountered, such as our example story, *Teddy Bears' Moving Day* by Susanna Gretz (A & C Black).

• The teddies begin the day squashed in their bed. It looks very comfortable, but rather cramped. Can the children make a warm, soft bed for Robert alone?
Teachers' notes: A selection of junk materials is needed.

Questions: Is the bed large enough? Can they tuck Robert in? Is the bed warm and soft? Can they make it softer?

• The heavy boxes are loaded into the removal van. Can the children discover which is the heaviest box?
Teachers' notes: Five boxes of varying weights are needed.
Questions: Can the children order the boxes by weight? Which is the largest box? Is the largest box the heaviest? Is the smallest one the lightest?

• Robert needs to pack his belongings. Help by packing the groceries in the box.
Teachers' notes: A cardboard box and an assortment of food packages are needed, including fragile items, plastic bottles and yoghurt pots.
Questions: What is the largest number of packages that will fit into the box? Is it easy to lift? Can the children close the lid? Do they have to pack the box in a special way?

• The bears leave the house; they have a map to show them the way. Can the children make a map to get from their classroom to the playground?
Teachers' notes: A copy of Charles' map is needed.
Questions: Can the children's friends follow their map? What features help identify the route? Is Charles' map helpful? Does it need to be changed?

• Robert has to go back to pick up the items he has dropped. Leave a trail of items along a route for a friend to follow.
Teachers' notes: Junk materials, modelling clay or Plasticine and matchboxes are needed. Blue glass can be simulated by colouring a piece of acetate sheet with OHP pen.
Questions: Which item was dropped first, and which last? How many items were dropped? Ask the children to make the items. Can they find a box to fit them in? Why did Robert drop the things?

• Charles needs a hot bath. Collect some items that he could have in his bath.
Teachers' notes: Provide some floating and sinking objects and a bowl of water.
Questions: Which items float and which sink? Do any float and then sink?

• The bears tidy the house. Can the children make a room for them, with furniture?
Teachers' notes: Use a box and some small junk items.

Questions: Can all five bears sit down in the room? Is there room for the spotty dog? Can the children invent a game for the bears to play in the room?

• Robert is out in his tent sulking. Can the children make a tent for him?

Teachers' notes: Fabric, string and sticks are needed.

Questions: Can Robert stand up in the tent? Will all his treasures fit in with him?

• The bears are having spaghetti for supper. Ask the children to plan a meal.

Teachers' notes: Paper plates and a variety of materials are needed.

Questions: Which is the most popular food? What time of the day would they eat their meal?

Puzzles

Puzzles can also be used to stimulate mathematical thinking. They are usually not open ended, but have a final solution. They are often printed in puzzle books, logic problem books and in newspapers and magazines. It is best to try them yourself first to check the level of difficulty. Also be aware that some children find it extremely frustrating if they are unable to solve a problem; these children may be better working on a more open-ended activity with no one 'correct' answer.

a. Rescue the cat
Age range: five to eight.
Group size: pairs.
What you need:
photocopiable pages 172-174.
What to do: Ask the children to cut out the ladders from page 173 and find the ladder that just reaches from the ground to each cat's body. They should then stick the ladders on to the sheet so that all the cats can be rescued.

The children can then use the spare ladders and the trees and cats on page 174 to make another puzzle for their friends or parents.

b. Fit them together
Age range: seven to ten.
Group size: pairs.
What you need:
photocopiable pages 175-176.
What to do: Let the children cut out the shapes on the right-hand side of page 175. They can then fit them together with the shapes on the left-hand side of the page to make two squares, a rectangle, a triangle and a parallelogram.

The children can use the shapes on page 176 to make a similar puzzle for their friends or their parents.

c. Routes
Age range: nine to thirteen.
Group size: pairs.
What you need:
photocopiable pages 177-178.
What to do: Ask the children to follow the networks on the sheet, making a single trip that starts at any dot and only travels over each line once.

Let them try the more complicated networks (they can both be solved).

CHAPTER 7

Managing the curriculum and assessment

Recording and assessment are terms that are often linked. However, it is important to recognise that they have different roles.

Assessment involves interaction between the teacher and the child, and is an integral part of the learning process.

Recording has three aspects:
• It is an aid for the teacher in forward planning.
• It is a management tool in the classroom for both the teacher and the child.
• It is an acknowledgement of the child's achievement.

At the heart of the process are the teacher and the child, and the teacher's assessment of the child's achievement. Recording is mainly utilitarian and should not become burdensome or clumsy. Learning is not dependent on a superb recording system, but it can be assisted by efficient recording by the teacher.

RECORDING

Records of planning

It is important to keep a check on curriculum coverage when planning. A broad view of a year's mathematics curriculum can be kept on photocopiable page 179.

It is not necessary to cover all the Attainment Targets every term; once a year should be enough.

Attainment Targets 1 and 9 cannot be considered in isolation; they can only occur through the other attainment targets. They therefore need a different approach at the planning stage. This can be recorded on photocopiable page 180.

A T	Term 1	Term 2	Term 3
AT2	Scheme		
AT3	Calculators		
AT4	Topic 'Foods'		
AT5	Calculators		
AT6			
AT7	N/A		
AT8	Christmas		
AT10	PE		
AT11	Topic 'Foods'		
AT12			
AT13			
AT14			

	AT1		AT9	
	AT2 AT3 AT4 AT5 AT6 AT7 AT8		AT10 AT11 AT12 AT13 AT14	
Period 1	Calculator investigative tasks		Data handling from topic 'Foods'	
	AT2 AT3 AT4 AT5 AT6 AT7 AT8		AT10 AT11 AT12 AT13 AT14	
Period 2	Calculator investigative tasks		Shape investigation from theme 'Christmas'	
	AT2 AT3 AT4 AT5 AT6 AT7 AT8		AT10 AT11 AT12 AT13 AT14	
Period 3	Scale plans from topic 'Our school'		Mapping from topic 'Our school'	
	AT2 AT3 AT4 AT5 AT6 AT7 AT8		AT10 AT11 AT12 AT13 AT14	
Period 4				
	AT2 AT3 AT4 AT5 AT6 AT7 AT8		AT10 AT11 AT12 AT13 AT14	
Period 5				
	AT2 AT3 AT4 AT5 AT6 AT7 AT8		AT10 AT11 AT12 AT13 AT14	
Period 6				

Recording management

Simple matrices listing various activities can be given directly to the children. This encourages independence and self-confidence in the children, and allows you more time to deal with the areas where help is most needed. Children who operate with this system also enjoy a degree of flexibility in their learning, and are motivated by being able to recognise exactly what is expected of them. These matrices can take many forms and a few examples are provided below and on photopiable pages 181-185.

This child has coloured the carriages as she has completed the tasks. The matrix forms a record for both the child and the teacher.

The flower petals can be shaded as the activities are completed.

The snake can be filled in as activities are allocated to the child.

The child who filled in the chart opposite has crossed out the completed activities.

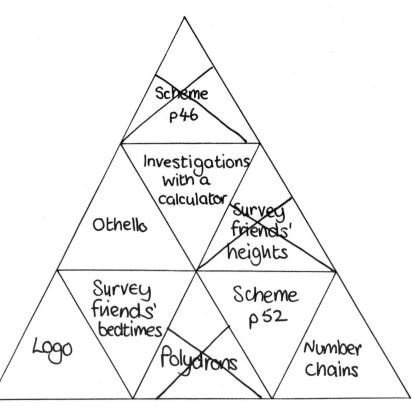

The above matrix can also be completed as the child works through the programme.

ASSESSMENT

Why assess?

It is essential to assess in order to:
• identify what the child can do;
• discover what the child is learning;
• establish the child's needs in order to progress;
• inform others.

You need to be informed about the knowledge, concepts and skills that the child has and is able to apply in practical situations.

Sensitive assessment also enables you to have a clearer view of what the child is actually learning when you are planning the curriculum. This has a greater value than discovering what a child can already do.

It is also important to establish the child's needs as there are many occasions when a child is engaged in an activity when there is a need to extend her knowledge or skills. It is necessary to identify these moments and provide opportunities for needs to be met.

We all have a legal requirement to report on the children's progress to others, both internally and externally to the school.
• Internally to the child, other teachers, the headteacher, the parents and the governors.
• Externally to the child's next school and to the LEA.

What to assess?

It is important to gain a picture of the whole child. This means that you will need to take a broader focus than the mathematical knowledge acquired. We can assess all of the five elements of learning – knowledge, concepts, strategies, skills and attitudes.

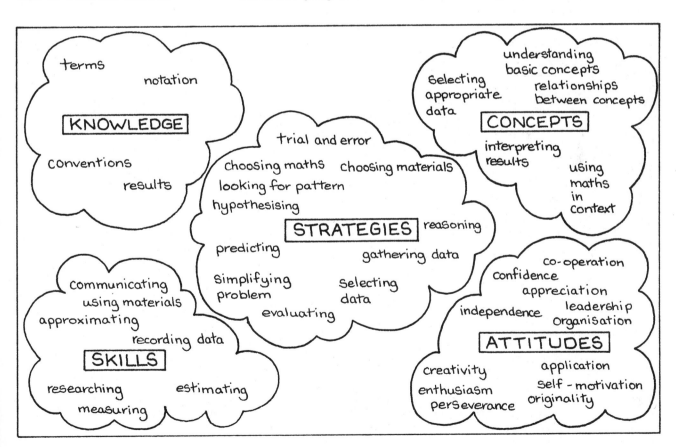

When to assess?

Formative assessment is a continuous process, and is a way of identifying the next steps a child needs to take. There are times when a child has made a breakthrough in understanding or has mastered a skill that also needs to be assessed. It will be clear when these critical points occur.

Summative assessment, which informs you of a child's achievement, will be necessary as projects draw to a close or at the end of a term or year. This will take the form of a reflective overview rather than a series of assessment tasks. It is a process in which the child can be involved.

How to assess?

Assessment should be an integral part of all teaching and learning. Teachers have a wide range of methods available to them and it is important to use these methods flexibly and to choose methods which are appropriate to the particular situation.

The following are some of the possible methods of assessment.

- Discussion: through discussion with a child or group of children it is possible to assess their understanding of ideas, their ability to communicate mathematics and pass on knowledge, their attitudes to the task and their social interaction. A two-minute chat can reveal a great deal.
- Questioning: by asking specific questions it is possible to see what a child has learnt. Open-ended questions tend to be the most revealing, allowing children a greater chance to demonstrate their abilities. Introduce variable questions to allow the children to hypothesise. Challenge children by asking questions such as 'What would happen if...?'
- Observation: this can be very brief; a glance across the classroom is often enough. More structured observation methods include standing back from the class for two or three minutes, and observing one child or a group of children a number of times throughout the day, taking notes of critical or unusual events and observing the outcome of the task.
- Listening: carry out assessment by eavesdropping on informal discussions, or listening to the brainstorming of a problem.
- Child self-evaluation: it is important to encourage the children to evaluate their own work. Take the children's evaluation into account in the assessment.
- Recorded work: this provides tangible evidence for which the assessment can be delayed. It is sometimes useful, however, to note comments relevant to the work while it is in progress, or soon afterwards.

Most mathematics schemes provide 'end of level' tests which can be used as part of a summative assessment. Many teachers have also identified open-ended tasks that provide a form of summative assessment.

Recording assessment

The recording of assessment tends to 'mushroom'. It should not be allowed to take over or be an unnecessary burden for you. Reams of uninformative recording sheets or checklists are a waste of your time and take up a lot of space. It is important to think carefully about the purpose of the recording, and whether it is useful and informative.

It is not useful to keep files full of outdated work; what is necessary is a record of recent and relevant mathematics. These records can be kept in small folders and updated as appropriate, probably once a term. Intangible evidence can also be included through notes and jottings. Photocopiable page 186 can be used to record children's comments and discussion; this could also be kept in the folder.

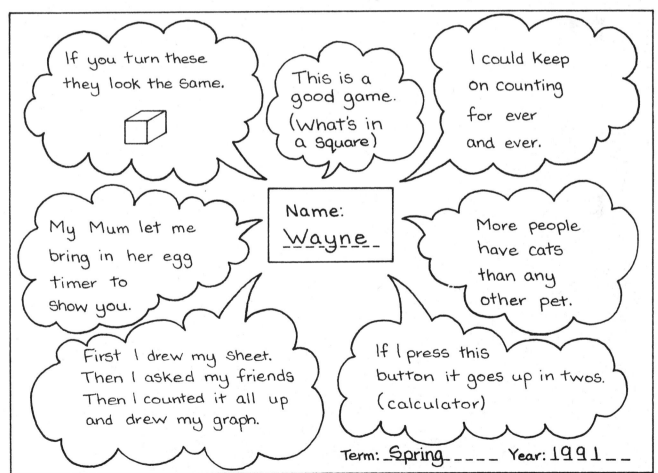

A record of the five elements of learning can be kept on photocopiable page 187. This should be a reflective record that highlights the child's involvement with the task. Cross-reference can be made to particular pieces of work in the folder. It is useful to number the items for ease of identification.

Each assessment period will reveal different aspects of each of the five areas of learning and experience. A further valuable piece of evidence is a child's own evaluation of a project or topic. Photocopiable page 188 provides a framework which the children could complete, or on which the teacher could record oral comments made by the children.

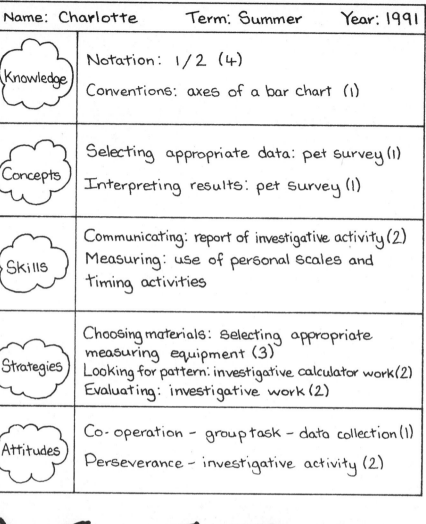

Name: Charlotte	Term: Summer	Year: 1991

Knowledge	Notation: 1/2 (4) Conventions: axes of a bar chart (1)
Concepts	Selecting appropriate data: pet survey (1) Interpreting results: pet survey (1)
Skills	Communicating: report of investigative activity (2) Measuring: use of personal scales and timing activities
Strategies	Choosing materials: Selecting appropriate measuring equipment (3) Looking for pattern: investigative calculator work (2) Evaluating: investigative work (2)
Attitudes	Co-operation – group task – data collection (1) Perseverance – investigative activity (2)

Photocopiable pages 189 and 190 provide a framework for recording a child's progress through the National Curriculum in terms of the statements of attainment. This conforms to the legal requirement, but only provides a small part of the necessary information for assessment.

It is possible to complete these pages either as a simple checklist:

or making reference to particular pieces of work in the folder by using the cross-referencing number system (see opposite).

It is important to make your record keeping as useful and easy to use as possible. It should fit in with your way of working. Try not to accumulate superfluous material; make your recording serve a purpose and work for you.

CHAPTER 8

Resources

In order to make the classroom a stimulating environment for mathematics, a wide range of resources can be used. These do not have to be commercially produced or very expensive, as in fact more interest may be stimulated by ordinary junk materials than by the most costly apparatus.

We have identified seven main categories of resources.
• General – paper and stationery etc;
• Materials for the preparation of teaching aids – templates, rubber stamps etc;

• Specialised equipment – Base 10, Multilink etc;
• Everyday equipment – balances, clocks, calculators etc;
• Collected resources – junk, natural materials etc;
• Games and software – general and specialised;
• Books – for teachers and for children.

Resources can be used by groups or individuals, and can be organised in four main ways:
• in the classroom, available to the children;
• shared between a few classes;
• in a central area in the school, such as the staff library;

• shared between a group of schools, in the case of expensive items like computers.

Periodically, it is worth taking an inventory to check the location and condition of the school's mathematics resources. Broken balances in the back of a cupboard help nobody.

There follows a list of some of the resources from each of the seven categories which we have found to be the most useful. The relevant resources have also been listed at the end of each chapter.

General

- Rulers: preferably transparent plastic and clearly marked in centimetres.
- Scissors: sharp but with rounded ends. Some provision should be made for left-handed children.
- Pencils: HB for normal use, but mathematical construction requires a harder point – at least 2H. Older children can produce very good results using 0.5mm propelling pencils.
- Compasses: Mathematical construction requires good quality spring bow compasses, but cheaper compasses that take normal pencils are suitable for less accurate work.
- Construction paper: this is for making nets etc. It should be thick, smooth and strong.
- Drawing paper: this is for mathematical construction, and needs to be smooth and quite thick, like cartridge paper.
- Plain paper: this is for recording.
- Squared paper: 20mm, 10mm, 5mm and 2mm.
- Tracing paper: this needs to be strong.
- Gummed paper: assorted bright colours.
- Paper fasteners: for turning shapes, Geostrips etc.
- Elastic bands: assorted for Geo Boards.

Preparation materials

- Rubber stamps: shapes, money, pictures, clock faces.
- Gummed shapes: coins, geometric shapes.
- Stencils: shapes.
- Templates: shapes.
- Blank playing cards: available from E. J. Arnold.
- Wrapping paper, magazines and calendars: for pictures.

NB All of the above should also be available to the children for use during mathematical exploration.

Specialised mathematical resources

- Base 10 materials: plastic or wooden.
- Multilink or possibly Unifix.
- Centicubes.
- Number tracks and lines: 1-10 and 1-100.
- Number squares: 1-9, 1-25, 1-100.
- Counting materials: counters etc.
- Pegboards.
- Geo Boards: pin, 25 pin, isometric.
- Geo Strips.
- Logic materials: Logic Blocks, Animal and Transport Allsorts, Logic People, Treesorts, Seasorts, Housesorts, attribute cylinders.
- Sorting trays.
- Two-dimensional shapes: including irregular shapes and also Clixi or Polydron.
- Three-dimensional shapes: wooden or plastic.
- Probability kit (not essential).

Everyday resources

- Threading beads.
- Linear measure: 30cm rulers, metre sticks, steel tapes, 30m tapes, trundle wheels (not essential), height measure, tape-measures.
- Mass measure: scales (personal and kitchen balances, spring balances), masses (iron, brass, plastic).
- Capacity measure: measuring cylinders, measuring spoons, displacement bucket, volume conservation set, sand and water trays and equipment, funnel.
- Time measure: sand-timers, egg-timers, analogue clock, digital clocks, stop watch, stop clock, calendar.

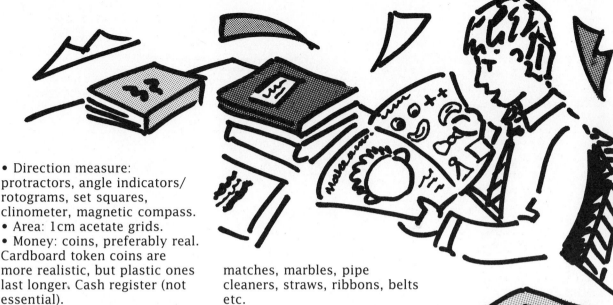

- Direction measure: protractors, angle indicators/ rotograms, set squares, clinometer, magnetic compass.
- Area: 1cm acetate grids.
- Money: coins, preferably real. Cardboard token coins are more realistic, but plastic ones last longer. Cash register (not essential).
- Calculators: simple four-function calculators, with memory.
- Dice: a range of shapes and sizes, including blanks.
- Dominoes: with numbers and with pictures.
- Playing cards.
- Mirrors: preferably plastic.
- Spinners: in a range of shapes.

Collected resources

- Packaging: a series of similar shapes (possibly a range of small, medium and large boxes from the same product), a set of containers with different shapes but the same capacity perhaps shampoo bottles), interesting polyhedra (for example, Toblerone or Biarritz boxes), tubs and containers (some with lids), items for the class shop.
- Natural materials: small pebbles, fir cones, acorns, conkers, nuts, shells, twigs, sand etc.
- Balloons: a range of shapes, sizes and colours.
- Arbitrary measures: cups, spoons, jugs, headless

matches, marbles, pipe cleaners, straws, ribbons, belts etc.
- Plasticine or clay.
- Pictures: from calendars, magazine, brochures, greetings cards etc.

Games and software

- Specialist games: for example, 'What's in the square', 'What else is in the square', 'Equality', 'Mr Money Game'.
- General games: for example, snakes and ladders, Mastermind, Connect 4, Othello, Take 10.
- Specialist software: for example, *Shiva*, *Smile* and simulation producers.
- General software: for example, spread sheets, data bases, Logo.

Books

For the teacher/staff library
- *Bounce to it* (infants), Gillian Hatch (Manchester Polytechnic)
- *Bright Ideas Maths* Activities, Julia Matthews (ed) (Scholastic Publications, 1985)
- *Bright Ideas Maths Games*, Rosemarie Brewer and Marion Cranmer (Scholastic Publications, 1988).

- *Children and Number*, Martin Hughes (Blackwell).
- *How Children Learn Mathematics*, Pamela Liebeck (Penguin, 1984).
- *I don't know, let's find out*, Wendy Garrard (Suffolk County Council).
- *Investigations in Mathematics*, Lorraine Mottershead (Blackwell).
- *Jump to it* (9-14 years), Gillian Hatch (Manchester Polytechnic).
- *Leap to it* (9-14 years), Gillian Hatch (Manchester Polytechnic).
- *Let's Investigate Handling Data*, Books 1, 2 and 3, Jean Haigh and Beryl Webber (Scholastic Publications, 1990).
- *Let's Investigate Numbers*, Books 1, 2 and 3, Beryl Webber and Jean Haigh (Scholastic Publications, 1989).

• *Let's Investigate Patterns*,
Books 1, 2 and 3, Jean Haigh
and Beryl Webber (Scholastic
Publications, 1989).
• *Let's Investigate Shapes*,
Books 1, 2 and 3, Beryl Webber
and Jean Haigh (Scholastic
Publications, 1988).
• *Mathematical Activities*, Brian
Bolt (CUP, 1982).
• *More Mathematical Activities*,
Brian Bolt (CUP, 1985).
• *Even More Mathematical
Activities*, Brian Bolt (CUP).
• *Mathematics Counts*, Dr W.H.
Cockcroft (HMSO).
• *Mathematics from 5 to 16*
(DES/HMSO).
• *Mathematics in ILEA Primary
Schools*, Parts 1 and 2 (ILEA).
• *Mathematics in the National
Curriculum* (DES/WO, 1989).
• *Maths Talk,* Mathematical
Association (Stanley Thornes).
• *Primary Mathematics Today*,
Elizabeth Williams and Hilary
Shuard (Longman, 1983).
• *Primary Mathematics Today
and Tomorrow*, Hilary Shuard
(Longman, 1988).
• *Sharing Maths with Parents*,
Mathematical Association
(Stanley Thornes).
• *Sources of Mathematical
Discovery*, Lorraine
Mottershead (Blackwell, 1979)

• *Teachers Handbooks – Maths*
(Scholastic Publications, 1987).
• *Teaching Mathematics to
Young Children*, D. Thyer and
J. Maggs (Holt, 1981).
• *Thinking Things Through*,
Leone Burton (Blackwell).
• *A Way with Mathematics*,
Nigel Langdon and Charles
Snape (CUP, 1984).

Books for children
Mathematical books for
children can be separated into
two main categories – those
which provide specialised
mathematical information, and
general story books which can
be starting points for problem
solving activities.
• Information books:
Annette, Marion Walter (Andre
Deutsch, 1971).
*Another, another & more
Bronto Books Sets A-E*, Eric
Albany (ed), (Longman).
Investigating... series, Catherall
(ed) (Wayland).
• Story books:
Each Peach Pear Plum, Janet
and Alan Ahlbeg (Fontana).
The Enormous Crocodile, Roald
Dahl (Puffin).
Funny Bones, Janet and Alan
Ahlberg (Fontana).
The Jolly Postman, Janet and
Alan Ahlberg (Heinemann).
The *Spot* series, Eric Hill
(Puffin).
The *Teddy Bear* series,
Suzannah Gretz (A & C Black).

Further points
Most mathematical apparatus
is self-explanatory, but some
items in particular have
enormous potential in an active
primary classroom. We shall
therefore discuss these further.

Number materials
• Cuisenaire Rods and Colour
Factor: these rods have been
available for a number of
years, but have declined in
popularity recently. The two
types are not interchangeable,
as they use a different colour
coding system. More recent
apparatus such as Multilink
probably has more value in
developing number concepts,
but Cuisenaire and Colour
Factor can still be used
profitably as a resource for
investigative activities, and in
exploring ideas of area,
fractions and shape and
number patterns.
• Unifix: these plastic pieces
are basically 2cm cubes. They
join together in one way only,
which limits their use in areas
of mathematics other than
number and linear measure.

They are brightly coloured and attractive to children. The manufacturers also supply other pieces of apparatus to support their use, like number tracks.

• Multilink: these plastic pieces are also basically 2cm cubes, and are brightly coloured. Their advantage over Unifix is that they link together in all directions. The joining method means that they are slightly more difficult to separate than Unifix, but usually they can be handled easily even by very young children. The multi-directional joining does mean that Multilink can be used in many areas of the mathematics curriculum, including shape.

Again the manufacturers provide a wide range of support materials to accompany Multilink, including some National Curriculum materials.

New shapes are being added to the range, including 'prisms' and 'isos', and this widens the variety of three-dimensional shapes that can be built. There is also a range of materials for older children, including secondary pupils, which includes Advanced Multilink, an equivalent set of black, white and grey cubes.
• Centicubes: these are 1cm plastic cubes which join in all directions and are also brightly coloured. The main disadvantage is that they are quite difficult to separate; they are therefore only suitable for older pupils.

They have particular value for volume and weight activities as they measure $1cm^2$ and weigh 1 gram.
• Number base material: this material is available in a variety of number bases, but

base ten is the most useful, as our number system is denary, and grouping in other bases is possible using other materials.

Number base material is available in wood or plastic. Multibase is made of plastic, and is colour-coded for the various base numbers.

Base ten material is particularly valuable as an aid to understanding place value and to help with performing number operations. It has a key role to play in every classroom

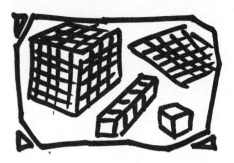

where place value has been introduced. Base ten material can also be used as a basis for many number games involving exchange.
• Calculators: simple four-function calculators with a memory are a vital tool in mathematics. They should be available in every classroom, and should be used in a variety of ways.

The skills of using a calculator should be taught throughout the primary phase in order to promote sensible and efficient use of the machine.

Calculators can be used to develop understanding, and as an aid to exploration. They also help with problem solving and investigative work, as real data may be troublesome to handle, and patterns can be identified more easily if the drudgery of the arithmetic has been removed.

Logic materials
Logical thought is the basis of mathematics and structured sets of apparatus provide opportunities for sorting, classification, deduction and conclusion. Logic materials have a part to play in the mathematical experience of primary pupils of all ages. Attribute cards, spinners and dice can extend the range of possibilities of the materials.

Structured sets contain a number of totally unique pieces that cover all possible combinations of attributes. The sets vary in complexity and number of pieces. Free play must be allowed before the structured use of these materials.

• Animal/Transport Allsorts (two attributes); 6 shapes × 6 colours = 36 pieces.

• Seasorts (two attributes); 8 pictures × 8 colours = 64 pieces.

• Treesorts (three attributes); 5 shapes × 6 colours × 2 textures = 60 pieces.

• Logic People (four attributes); 2 sexes × 2 ages × 4 colours × 3 positions = 48 pieces.

• Logic Blocks (four attributes); either 4 shapes × 3 colours × 2 thicknesses × 2 sizes = 48 pieces; or 5 shapes × 3 colours × 2 thicknesses × 2 sizes = 60 pieces.

• Housesorts (four attributes); 3 heights × 3 windows × 2 chimneys × 4 colours = 72 pieces.

Shape materials
Two-dimensional shape
It must be remembered that no apparatus truly represents two dimensions, as all materials have depth. However, it is useful to have a set of plastic or cardboard plane shapes available to support activities such as tessellation, pattern

making and exploring symmetry. The set should include both regular and irregular shapes.

• Clixi: these plastic shapes fit together quite easily to enable children to build three-dimensional shapes. There is an ever-increasing range of shapes available.

• Polydrons: these shapes are similar to Clixi but are slightly more difficult to fit together. The three-dimensional shapes when built have a smoother outline than those built using Clixi.

• Polyshapes: these are cardboard shapes that can be joined together with elastic bands to form a wide variety of three-dimensional shapes. They are particularly challenging for older children, and can be used and reused many times.

Three-dimensional shapes
Both wooden and plastic shapes are available in sets, but these can be quite expensive.

• Poleidoblocs: a brightly coloured collection of wooden shapes that have relationships between their dimensions. This allows comparisons to be made. They form a structured set of shapes, the attributes being shape, colour and size.

• Construction straws: these are plastic straws of different lengths and colours that can be joined together to form the edges of three-dimensional shapes, allowing properties such as rotational symmetry and Euler's formula to be more easily explored.

Management of resources

The following are some important points to bear in mind.

• All resources should be openly available to the children.

• All resources should be easily available to the children.

• The children should know where all resources are kept.

• The children should be encouraged to decide which resources are appropriate.

• The children should be encouraged to decide when and if resources are appropriate.

• There should be no stigma attached to the use of resources at any time.

• The children should be encouraged to take care of the resources at all times.

CHAPTER 9

Glossary

The following glossary of terms is intended to be used as an aide-mémoire for teachers, or as a reference for any pupils who are able to read and assimilate the text for themselves. Each term is defined and illustrated with a diagram or illustration. The words in italics have separate listings in the glossary.

The only terms which have been defined are those which occur in the first six levels of the National Curriculum, and which, from experience, we have found to be confusing or unclear.

A

ANGLE is the turn from one line to another, when both lines meet at a point. Angles are measured in degrees.

• An acute angle is a sharp angle; a turn between 0° and 90°.

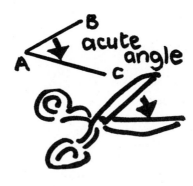

• An obtuse angle is a wide angle; a turn between 90° and 180°.

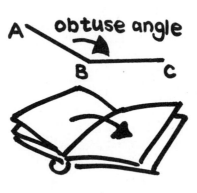

• A reflex angle is a very wide angle; a turn between 180° and 360°.

APPROXIMATION sets an amount within reasonable, flexible boundaries. It is useful for very large or small numbers, when complete accuracy is unnecessary. Approximation is based on numerical evidence, but this does not have to be precise.

approximate attendance. 17,000

eggs	52p
butter	63p
cereal	£1.09
baked beans	27p
	25p
Yoghurt	99p
cola	54p
milk	

50p + 60p + £1.10 + 30p + 20p + £1 + 50p = £4.20

actual cost £4.29

ASSUMPTIONS OF SYMMETRY are linked with *probability*. If after 20 throws of a die you had not thrown a six, assumptions of symmetry would lead you to believe that next time you are more likely to throw a six than any other number. Probability theory has it that on each occasion, each number has an equal chance of being thrown, regardless of what has gone before.

B

BAR CHARTS are used to communicate information of a *continuous* nature, for example, length, weight, and *capacity*. The scale is numbered on the lines and there is a position for zero. The height of the bars corresponds to the figure they represent.

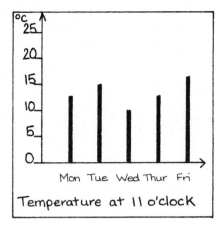

Temperature at 11 o'clock

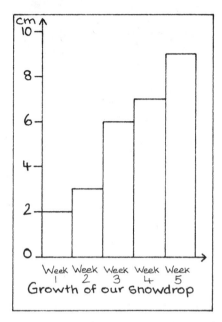

Growth of our snowdrop

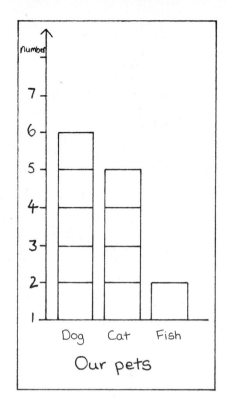

Our pets

A **BEARING** is the *angle* measured clockwise from north to the object sighted. They are always written in three *digits*. Bearings are used in navigation.

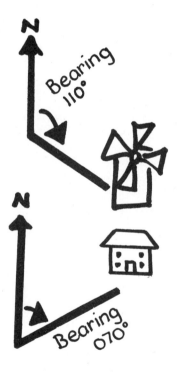

BAR LINE GRAPHS are used to communicate information of a *continuous* nature – for example, length, weight, *capacity* or temperature – against a *discrete* variable like a day, week or month.

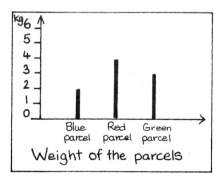

Weight of the parcels

BLOCK GRAPHS are used to communicate information which is *discrete*; for example, spoonfuls, number of people or shoe sizes. The scale is numbered in the spaces, and there is no position for zero.

C

CAPACITY is the amount of space available into which something may be poured or put. This can be the internal *volume* of a container like a vacuum flask or a car boot. The metric units of measurement for capacity include millilitres (ml), centilitres (cl), and litres (l). The imperial units of measurement include pints (pt) and gallons (gal).

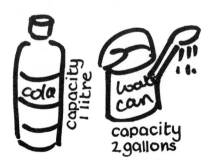

A **CARROLL DIAGRAM** is used to communicate information about a set of objects. The set will have been divided into a subset and its opposite (complement); for example, hot and not hot, long and not long, square and not square. This involves classifying by one criterion.

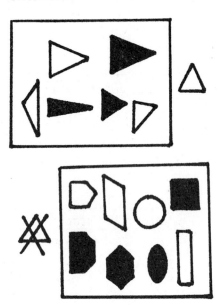

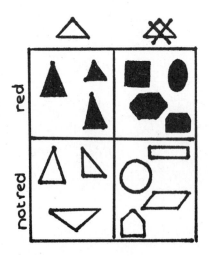

Classifying by two criteria gives four decisions; for example, triangle, not triangle, red, not red.

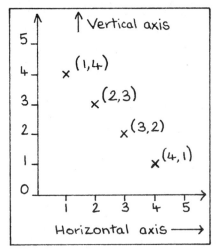

CARTESIAN CO-ORDINATES are used to describe position. A pair of numbers in order are enclosed in brackets. The first number describes position along the horizontal axis and the second number describes position along the vertical axis.

Cartesian co-ordinates describe position at a point, so the lines of the axes must be numbered and not the spaces.

A **COMPOUND MEASURE** is a measure which requires two or more units, for example, speed. Speed is calculated by dividing distance by time (km ÷ hours), and a compound unit is used (km/h or mph).

CONGRUENCE is when two objects or shapes have exactly the same dimensions, that is, the same shape and size.

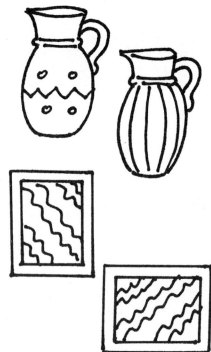

CONSERVATION OF A NUMBER is when a constant number of objects are placed in different arrangements but are still recognised to be the same number.

CONTINUOUS – See under *Variables*.

A **CONVERSION GRAPH** is used to convert information from one form to another. It shows the relationship between two sets of information.

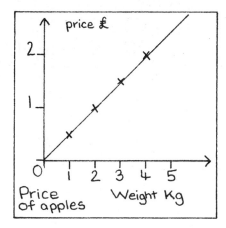

Price of apples

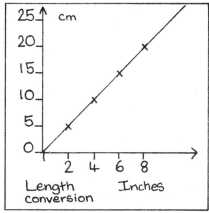

Length conversion

CORRELATION shows the relationship between two or more *variables*. It is a statistical process, and does not indicate whether one *variable* causes another. Thus 'umbrellas up' correlates with 'windscreen wipers on'.

John 7 years   John 17 years

Height correlates with weight

A **CYLINDER** is a circular-based prism.

D

DECIMAL NOTATION is used when amounts are recorded using a base ten system; for example, 11, 254, 15.7, 101.35. Decimal fractions are most frequently used with metric units of measurement.

- 1.64m is said 'one point six four metres' and is equivalent to 1 metre and 64 centimetres.
- 1.64kg is said 'one point six four kilograms' and is equivalent to 1 kilogram and 640 grams.
- £1.64 is said 'one pound sixty-four' and is equivalent to 1 pound and 64 pence.

DECIMAL PLACE is the position of a *digit* to the right of a decimal point.
- 2.4 – one decimal place (4).
- 3.75 – two decimal places (75).
- 10.319 – three decimal places (319).

The first decimal place represents tenths ($^1/_{10}$), the second hundredths ($^1/_{100}$) and the third thousandths ($^1/_{1000}$).

Moving a *digit* one decimal place to the left multiplies by ten.

0.4
4.0

Moving one decimal place to the right divides by ten.

6.1
0.61

A **DECISION TREE** is used to sort information, making decisions at every junction.

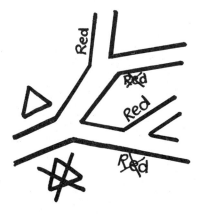

DIFFERENCE is when two sets are compared and matched one to one.

difference one

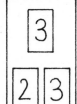

difference two

A **DIGIT** is a single symbol which forms all or part of a number.

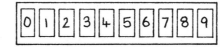

one-digit number – three

two-digit number – twenty-three

In decimal notation there are ten digits.

$$0\ 1\ 2\ 3\ 4\ 5\ 6\ 7\ 8\ 9$$

The value of the digit is determined by its position.

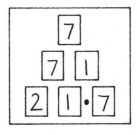

DISCRETE – See under *Variables*.

E

EQUAL CLASS INTERVALS is a method of handling data whereby a large amount of information is grouped together.

Symbols	Class interval	Frequency
£1	less than £1	III
£1≤f<£1.50	£1 up to £1.49	THH
£1.50≤f<£2.00	£1.50 up to £1.99	II
£2.00≤f<£2.50	£2.00 up to £2.49	THH I
£2.50≤f<£3.00	£2.50 up to £2.99	THH III
£3.00≤	£3 and over	II

Equal class intervals may be used with *discrete variables* (as above); or *continuous variables*, for example, height.

An **EQUATION** is a mathematical sentence balanced by an equals sign.

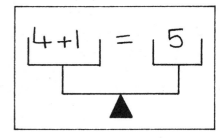

Equations can be purely numerical or algebraic.

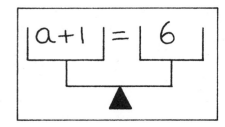

• A linear equation is when a straight line can be drawn to show the relationship between the *variables*. They are in the form mx + c = y, where m = gradient and c = a constant value; for example, 3x + 2 = y.

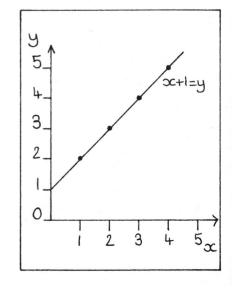

• Polynomial equations have more than one solution. These include a term which has been raised to a power; for example, $n^2 - 4 = m$, $2x^3 + 3xy + 2y^2 = 0$.

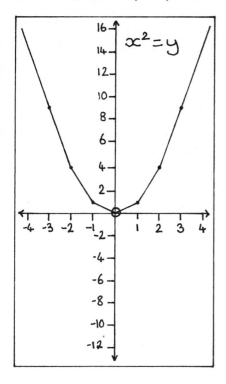

EQUIVALENCE is the state of being equal in value or amount.

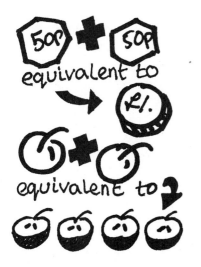

ESTIMATION is an educated guess based on previous experience.

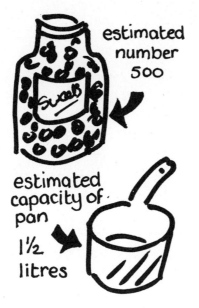

F,G,H

A **FACTOR** is a number which exactly divides into another number.

A **FORMULA** is a set pattern for calculating a *variable*. It is usually written using algebraic terms.

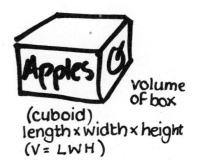

A **FREQUENCY** is how many times an event has taken place.

A **FREQUENCY DIAGRAM** is a type of *bar chart* where the height of the bar represents the *frequency*.

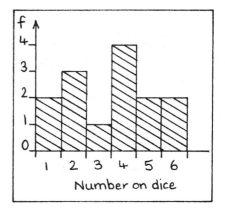

A **FREQUENCY TABLE** is a method of recording the *frequency* of an event.

Car colour	Tally	Frequency
Red	卌 卌 I	11
Blue	卌 III	8
Green	II	2
Black	卌 I	6

A **FUNCTION** is a relationship where there is a one to one correspondence like 'add four', 'multiply by two'.

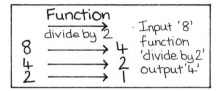

I,J,K

INDEX NOTATION is a method of writing numbers which indicates the times a number should be multiplied by itself.

$3^2 = 9$ (3×3)
$2^3 = 8$ $(2 \times 2 \times 2)$

An **INVERSE OPERATION** is the opposite to an operation (+, −, ×, ÷). The inverse of addition is subtraction and vice versa, and the inverse of multiplication is division and vice versa.

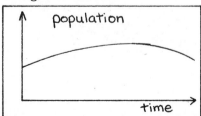

L

A **LINE GRAPH** is used to communicate the relationship between two *continuous variables*. The line may be straight or curved.

M

MAPPING is used to communicate a simple relationship. It may show a one-to-one or a many-to-one correspondence.

Where there is a one-to-many or many-to-many correspondence, the diagram is not strictly a mapping, but can be called an arrow diagram.

The **MEAN** is one way of calculating the average; it is not the only average. It is calculated by totalling all the values and dividing by the number of values.

Price of Apples	Month
25p	Jan
27p	Feb
27p	Mar
30p	Apr
31p	May
32p	June

25p + 27p + 27p + 30p + 31p + 32p = 172p
172p ÷ 6 = 28.67p
(average price from Jan to June)

A **MULTIPLE** is the product produced by multiplying a particular number a certain number of times.

N,O

A **NEGATIVE NUMBER** is a value that is less than zero. This has no concrete model, but is purely abstract.

A **NET** of a three-dimensional shape is the two-dimensional shape which, when cut out and folded, can be made into the three-dimensional shape.

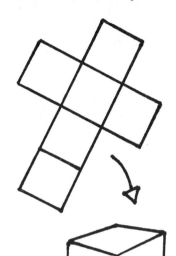

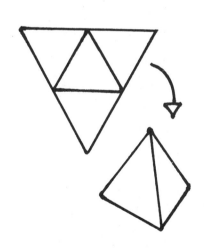

A **NETWORK** is a diagram of connected lines, for example, a London Underground map.

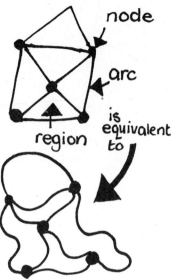

node

arc

region

is equivalent to

P

PARALLEL lines never meet, no matter how far they go. They always stay the same distance apart.

PERCENTAGE describes a fraction of an amount. The denominator of the fraction is 100.

$$\frac{1}{2} = \frac{50}{100} = 50\%$$

$$\frac{3}{4} = \frac{75}{100} = 75\%$$

$$1 = \frac{100}{100} = 100\%$$

PERPENDICULAR lines cross at right angles.

A **PICTOGRAM** is used to communicate large amounts of information in a pictorial form. One symbol is used to represent a number of units; for example, ten flowers. Half symbols are used to represent fewer units; for example, up to ten flowers, or half or more units; for example, from five to ten flowers.

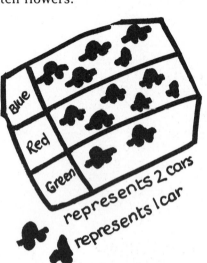

Pictograms can be used to show similar information to that shown in a *block graph*. They usually have no scale, but have a key to show what the symbol represents.

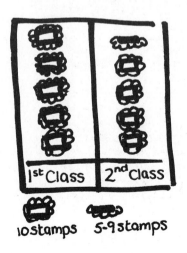

A **PIE CHART** is a way of communicating information about the parts of a whole; for example, how one day is spent, or how pocket money is spent. The chart is circular, and the sectors of the circle represent the information. It is easy to see the relative *proportions* of each category.

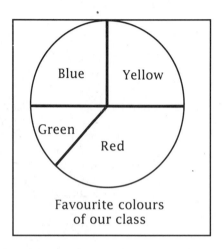

Favourite colours of our class

A **POLYGON** is a two-dimensional shape made up of straight lines. It may have three sides or more. A regular polygon has all sides and all *angles* equal. An irregular polygon has a variety of lengths of sides and *angles*.

Sides	Name
3	triangle
4	quadrilateral
5	pentagon
6	hexagon
7	heptagon
8	octagon
9	nonagon
10	decagon

• A triangle has three sides. The regular triangle is called equilateral. Triangles with two sides and two equal angles are called isosceles. Other triangles are called scalene.

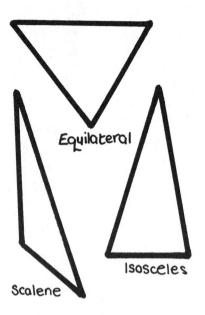

Triangles may also be described by their largest angle – acute, obtuse and right-angled.

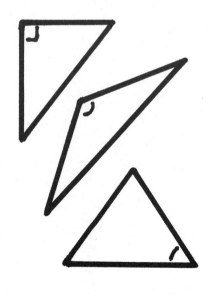

• A quadrilateral has four sides. The regular quadrilateral is a square. Quadrilaterals can be classified by their angles or their sides.

Some irregular quadrilaterals have special names:

Arrowhead

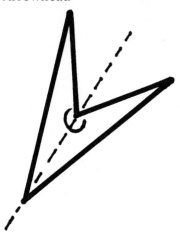

• one reflex angle;
• one line of symmetry

Kite

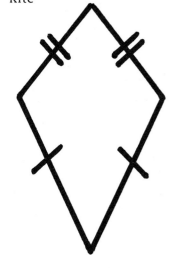

• two pairs of equal adjacent sides;
• diagonals are perpendicular;
• one line of symmetry.

Trapezium

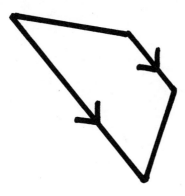

• one pair of parallel sides.

Parallelogram

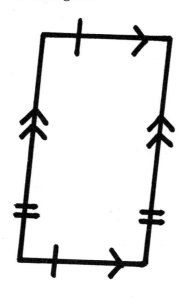

• two pairs of parallel sides;
• opposite sides are equal;
• opposite angles are equal;
• diagonals bisect each other;
• no lines of symmetry;
• rotational symmetry of order two.

Rhombus

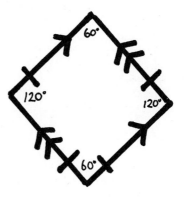

• two pairs of parallel sides;
• all sides are equal;
• opposite angles are equal;
• diagonals bisect at right angles;
• two lines of symmetry;
• rotational symmetry of order two.

Rectangle

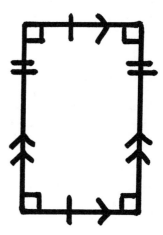

• two pairs of parallel sides;
• opposite sides are equal;
• all angles are 90°;
• diagonals are equal and bisect each other;
• two lines of symmetry;
• rotational symmetry of order two.

Oblong is the term for all rectangles that are not squares.

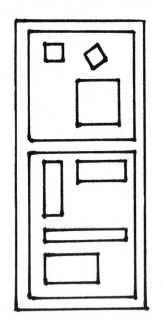

Square

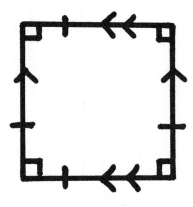

• two pairs of parallel sides;
• all sides are equal;
• all angles are 90°;
• diagonals are equal and bisect each other at right angles;
• there are four lines of symmetry;
• rotational symmetry of order four.

• A pentagon has five sides. The regular pentagon has equal sides and internal angles of 108°.

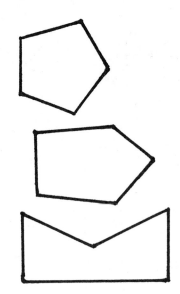

• A hexagon has six sides. The regular hexagon has equal sides and internal angles of 120°.

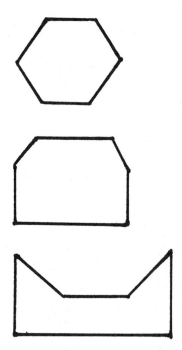

A **POLYHEDRON** is a solid shape with flat sides. There are five regular polyhedra. These are sometimes called Platonic solids. Prisms and pyramids are irregular polyhedra.

Regular polyhedra:

Cube

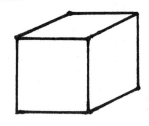

• six square faces;
• all the edges are equal in length.

Tetrahedron

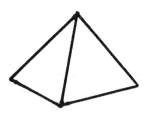

• four triangular faces;
• a regular tetrahedron has faces that are equilateral triangles.

Octahedron

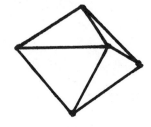

• eight triangular faces;
• a regular octahedron has faces that are equilateral triangles.

Dodecahedron

- twelve pentagonal faces;
- a regular dodecahedron has faces that are regular pentagons.

Icosahedron

- twenty triangular faces;
- a regular icosahedron has faces that are equilateral triangles.

A **prism** is a polyhedron that is the same shape all along its length. The base of a prism may be any shape.

A cuboid is a prism with a square or rectangular base; cuboids have six rectangular faces.

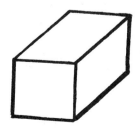

Triangular-based prism.

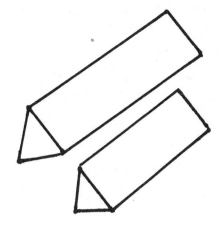

A **pyramid** is a polyhedron with a base which can be of any shape. All the other faces meet at a point, which may or may not be centrally placed above the base.

Triangular-based pyramid

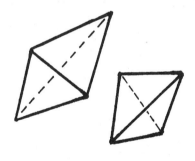

Square-based pyramid

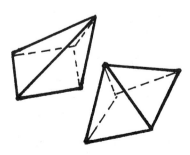

The **POWER** of a number is produced when a number has been multiplied by itself:

$$3 \times 3 = 9$$
$$3 \times 3 \times 3 = 27$$

3^4 can be said 'three to the power of four'.

PRIME numbers have only two *factors*, themselves and one.

$$37 \times 1 = 37$$

The number one is not a prime number, as it has only one *factor*.

The **PROBABILITY SCALE** ranges from 0 to 1. Probability describes the likelihood of an event happening.

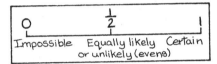

Sometimes probabilities are described as *percentages*.

PROPORTION is a relationship between one amount and another. Amounts are said to be in proportion if they increase or decrease with the same *scale factor*.

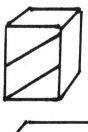

Q

A **QUADRANT** describes a quarter of a grid. The first quadrant refers to the positive quarter of a grid.

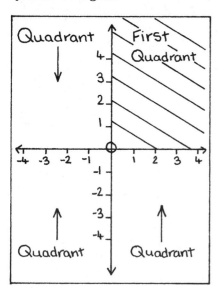

R

The **RANGE** is used to describe the difference between the highest and lowest values in a set of data.

Name	Shoe sizes
Julie	3
Andrew	6
Paul	7
Caroline	2
David	5

A **RATIO** is used to compare two amounts.

Ratios can be simplified like fractions – 10:4 simplifies to 5:2.

ROUNDING is a way of writing a number with fewer *digits* other than zero. This may make calculations easier. The amount by which the number has been rounded should be stated.

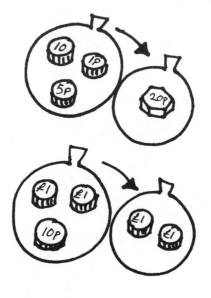

If the number ends in five or more, we round up; for example, 125 to the nearest ten is 130. If the number ends in four or below we round down; for example, 124 to the nearest ten is 120.

• Rounding errors happen when rounded numbers are used in calculations.

$$45 \times 13 = 585$$
rounded

$$50 \times 10 = 500$$
rounding error →85

S

The **SCALE FACTOR** is the amount by which a quantity or shape is increased or decreased. A whole number scale factor will increase the quantity.

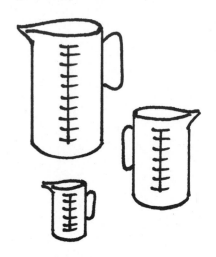

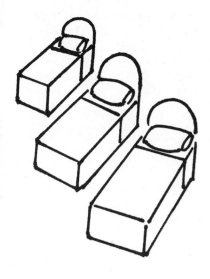

A **SPHERE** is a perfectly round three dimensional shape

• Reflection is when a shape is reflected about a line; this turns the shape over.

• Rotation is when a shape is turned about a point.

A **SCATTER GRAPH** is a way of communicating related information or information which illustrates trends.

T,U

TRANSFORMATION is the movement or alteration of a shape. Rotation, reflection and translation are transformations that alter not the dimensions of the shape but its position.

• Translation is when a shape moves along a line without turning.

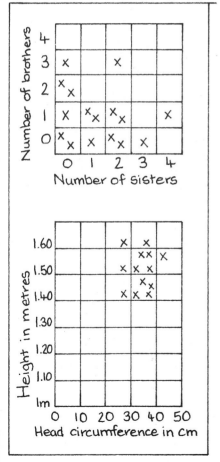

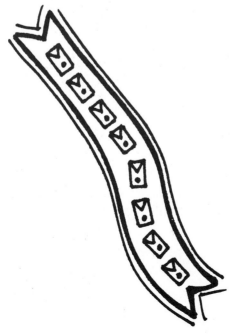

TWO-WAY TABLES can be used to collect data that can be classified in two different ways.

	Red	Yellow	Blue
Square	2	1	0
Circle	1	1	1
Triangle	0	2	1
Sorting our logic blocks			

	Tea	Coffee	Cola	Chocolate
Julie		✓	✓	
Andrew	✓			
Paul			✓	✓
Caroline	✓		✓	
David	✓			

Fillings

Bread		Jam	Cheese	Egg	Marmite
	Brown		✓	✓	✓
	White	✓	✓	✓	✓
	Granary		✓	✓	✓

V, W, X, Y, Z

VARIABLE describes an amount that can change.

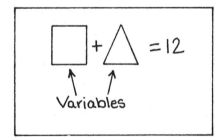

Variables

• 'Discrete variable' is used to describe a whole number variable that cannot be split continuously into many parts. For example, money – you can have £10 or £10.10 or £10.01 but not £10.0014. When a variable is discrete we can only use some points on a number line to represent it.

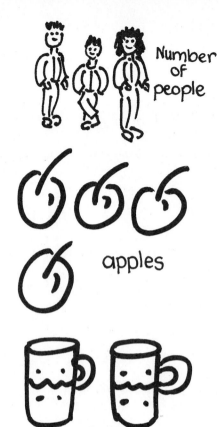

Number of people

apples

cupfuls

• Continuous variables can be any value, for example, speed, length, weight. When a variable is continuous we can use all points on a number line.

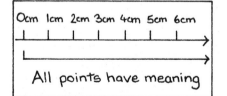

All points have meaning

A **VENN DIAGRAM** is used to communicate information about a set of objects. The set will have a subset identified. This involves classifying by one criterion.

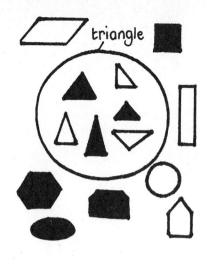

triangle

Classifying by two criteria gives four decisions.

red

triangle

VOLUME is the amount of space a solid takes up. The internal volume is the *capacity* of a container.

A T CHART

Use this chart to help match up the activities outlined in this book with the relevant National Curriculum attainment targets for mathematics. The activities are identified by numbers; thus **2/17** represents Chapter 2, activity 17.

LEVEL \ AT	1	2	3	4	5	6	7	8	9	10	11	12	13	14
1	1/1 1/5 1/8-9 3/1 6/a	1/1 1/5	1/1	1/8-9				3/1 6/a	4/2-3 4/6 5/1-2	4/6	4/2-3	5/1	5/2	
2	1/2-4 1/6 2/1-3 2/5-6 2/8 3/2 3/4-5	1/2-3	1/4-6 2/3 2/5	1/9	2/1-2 2/5 2/8	2/6		3/2 3/4-5	4/1-2 4/5 4/7 5/3-6	4/1 4/5 4/7	4/2	5/5	5/3-4	5/6
3	1/7 1/10 1/14 1/18 2/4 2/7-8 2/18 3/3 3/6	1/10	1/7 1/14 1/18	1/10	2/4 2/8 2/18	2/3 2/7		3/3 3/6 6/b	4/4 4/10 5/7 5/9	6/6	4/4 4/10			5/7 5/9
4	1/11-19 1/21 2/10-13 2/17-19 3/7-9 3/11-12	1/11-12 1/19 1/21	1/12-13 1/15-17	1/13	2/10-12 2/19	2/13 2/17	2/15	3/7-9 3/11-12 5/8	4/8-9 4/11-12 5/8	4/11-12	4/8-9			5/8
5	1/22-23 2/14-16 2/20-21 2/23 2/25 3/10 3/13-14		1/23	1/21-2	1/22 2/16 2/21 2/25	2/14-15 2/20 2/23		3/10 3/13-14	4/13-16 5/10 5/12-13 6/c	4/16	4/13-15 6/c	5/10	5/12-13	5/11
6	1/20 1/24	1/20	1/20	1/24					4/17	4/17				

PHOTOCOPIABLES

The pages in this section can be photocopied and adapted to suit your own needs and those of your class; they do not need to be declared in respect of any photocopying licence. Pages 138 to 178 each relate to a specific activitiy in the main body of the book, while pages 179 to 190 offer a range of formats to help with record-keeping and assessment. The appropriate activity and page references are given above each photocopiable sheet.

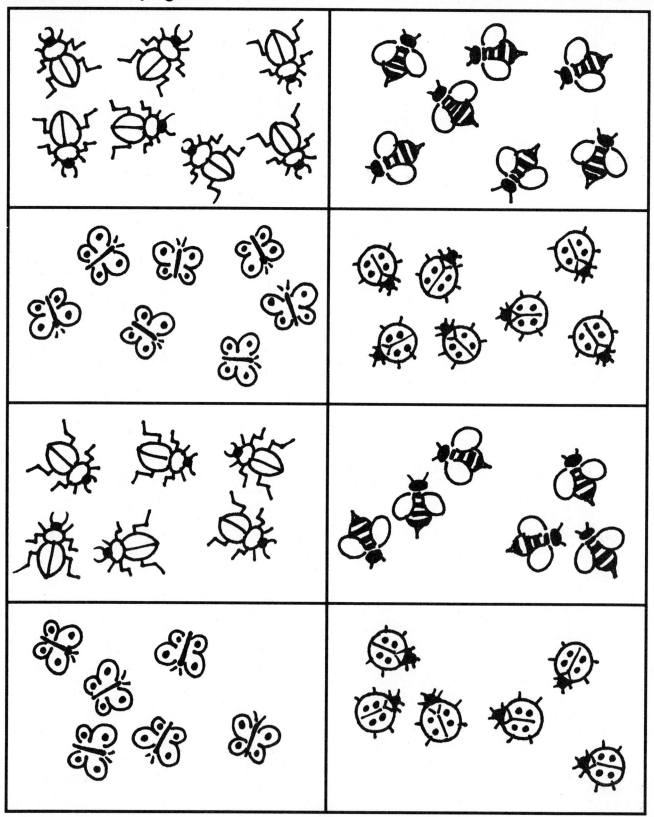

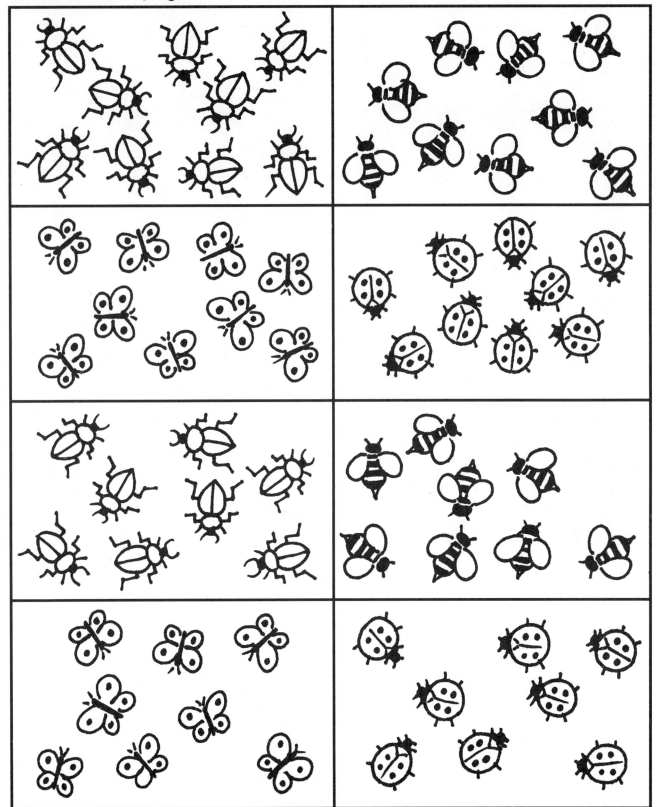

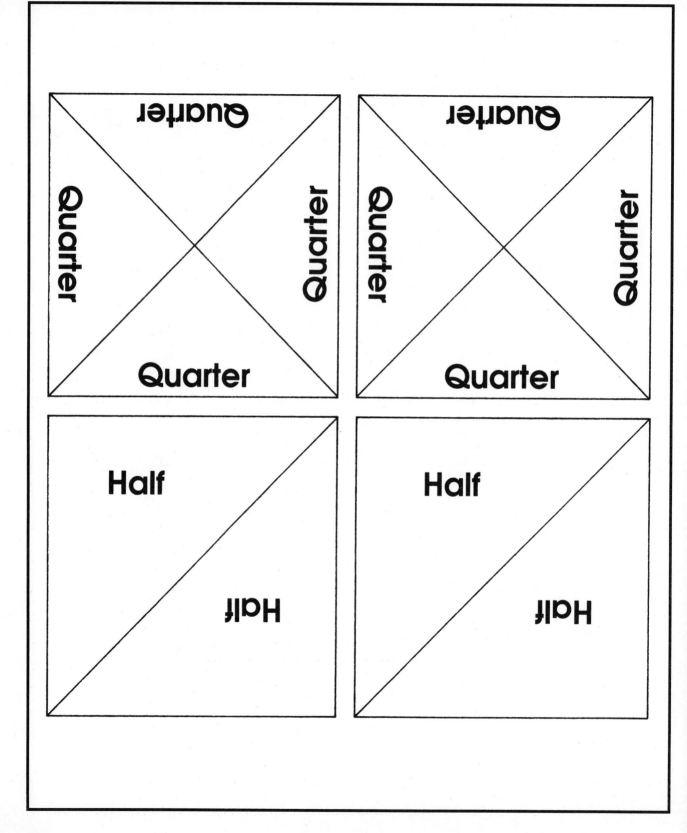

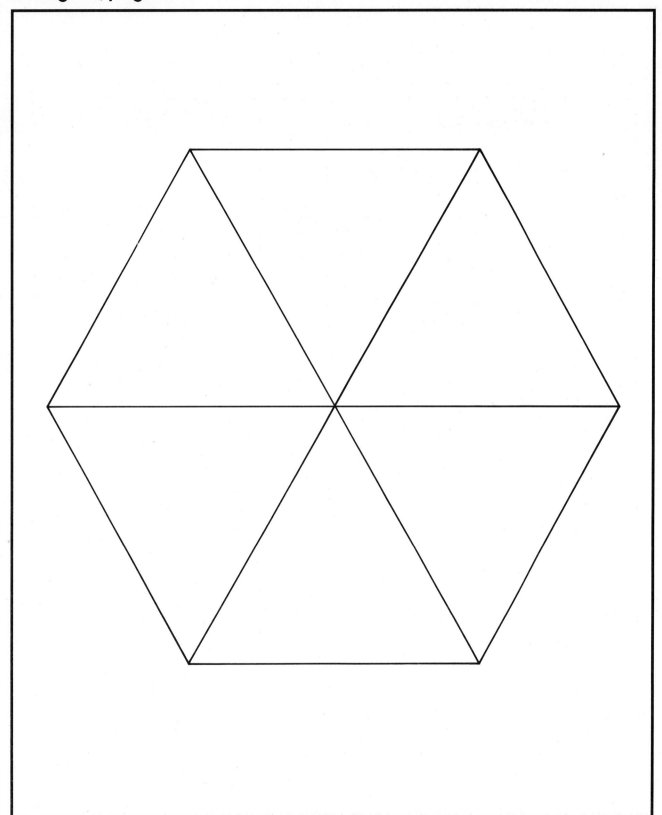

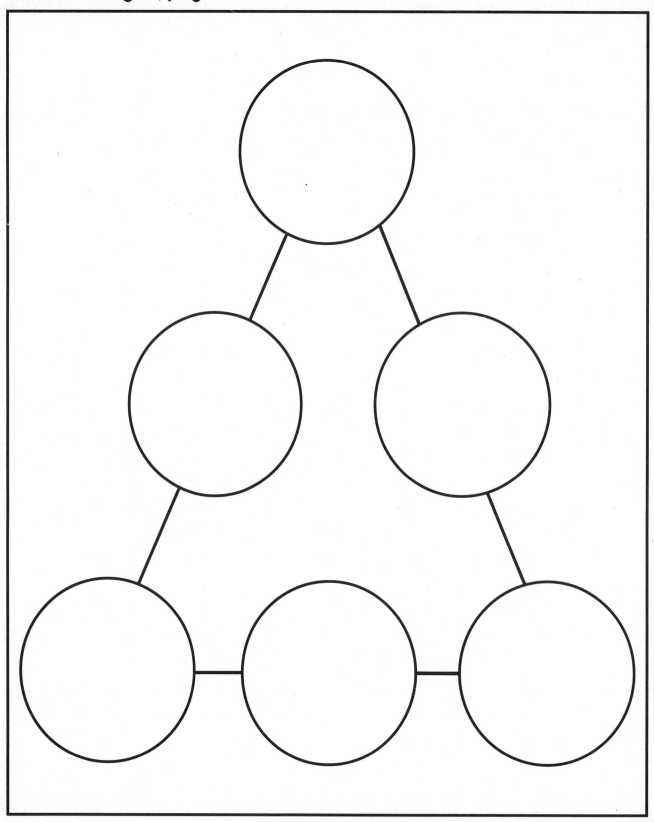

Fraction jigsaws, page 20

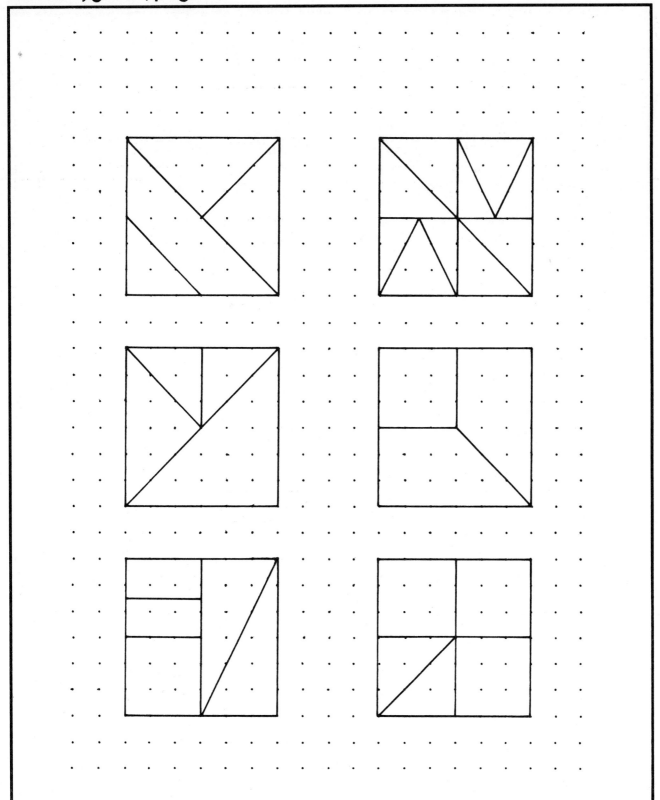

12	150	2	40	15	6
30	96	50	27	4	36
16	8	25	64	20	54
45	120	18	3	75	125
5	72	9	32	24	60
80	48	90	10	100	216

Place the numbers, page 23

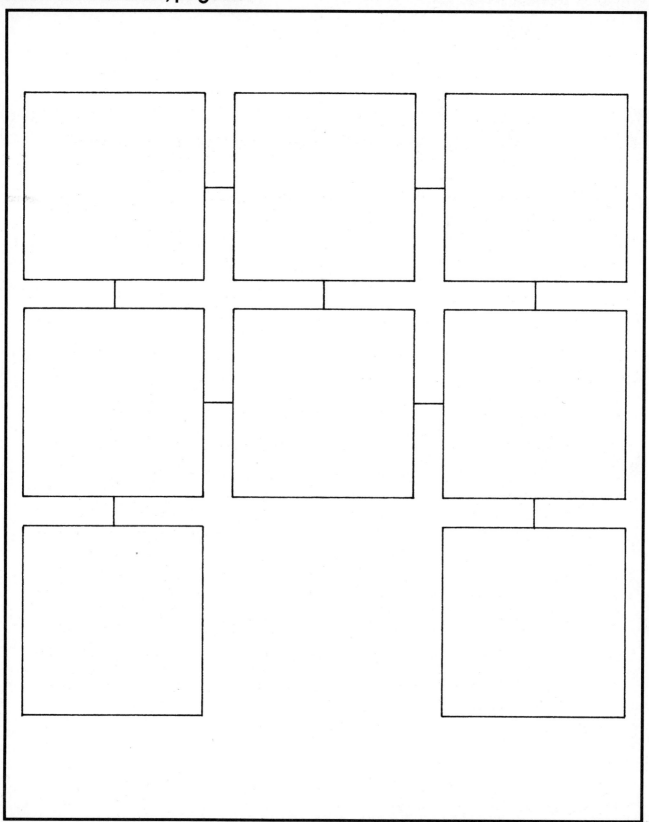

0.01	0.02	0.03	0.04	0.05	0.06	0.07	0.08	0.09	0.1
0.11	0.12	0.13	0.14	0.15	0.16	0.17	0.18	0.19	0.2
0.21	0.22	0.23	0.24	0.25	0.26	0.27	0.28	0.29	0.3
0.31	0.32	0.33	0.34	0.35	0.36	0.37	0.38	0.39	0.4
0.41	0.42	0.43	0.44	0.45	0.46	0.47	0.48	0.49	0.5
0.51	0.52	0.53	0.54	0.55	0.56	0.57	0.58	0.59	0.6
0.61	0.62	0.63	0.64	0.65	0.66	0.67	0.68	0.69	0.7
0.71	0.72	0.73	0.74	0.75	0.76	0.77	0.78	0.79	0.8
0.81	0.82	0.83	0.84	0.85	0.86	0.87	0.88	0.89	0.9
0.91	0.92	0.93	0.94	0.95	0.96	0.97	0.98	0.99	1

$\dfrac{1}{2}$	$1 \div 2$	0.5	50%
$\dfrac{1}{4}$	$1 \div 4$	0.25	25%
$\dfrac{1}{5}$	$1 \div 5$	0.2	20%
$\dfrac{1}{10}$	$1 \div 10$	0.1	10%
$\dfrac{3}{4}$	$3 \div 4$	0.75	75%

$\dfrac{2}{5}$	$2 \div 5$	0.4	40%
$\dfrac{3}{10}$	$3 \div 10$	0.3	30%
$\dfrac{4}{5}$	$4 \div 5$	0.8	80%
$\dfrac{7}{10}$	$7 \div 10$	0.7	70%
$\dfrac{9}{10}$	$9 \div 10$	0.9	90%

25 % of	$\frac{1}{5}$ of	$\frac{7}{8}$ of	50 % of	$\frac{2}{3}$ of	10 % of	$\frac{5}{6}$ of	$\frac{3}{4}$ of
4 8	6 5	1 6	5 0	6	20 0	1 0	2 0
15 % of	40 % of	45 % of	25 % of	100 % of	99 % of	$\frac{1}{2}$ of	75 % of
8 0	8 0	8 1	2 6	19 8	20 0	2 6	2 0
$\frac{3}{16}$ of	60 % of	$\frac{1}{2}$ of	$\frac{6}{7}$ of	$\frac{4}{9}$ of	200 % of	25 % of	70 % of
6 4	2 0	2 4	1 4	2 7	1 2	10 0	7 0
1% of	$\frac{1}{5}$ of	$\frac{3}{7}$ of	150 % of	$\frac{4}{5}$ of	10 % of	$\frac{3}{5}$ of	$\frac{3}{5}$ of
10 0	1 5	2 1	1 6	1 5	1 5	3 0	6 5
$\frac{2}{3}$ of	$\frac{1}{2}$ of	$\frac{3}{5}$ of	50 % of	$\frac{3}{4}$ of	20 % of	$\frac{7}{10}$ of	60 % of
2 7	1 9	2 5	15 0	1 6	5 0	7 0	3 0
$\frac{1}{2}$ of	60 % of	$\frac{1}{3}$ of	40 % of	$\frac{2}{3}$ of	40 % of	$\frac{1}{2}$ of	90 % of
9 0	8 0	1 5	2 4	1 8	3 6	5 0	1 8
15 % of	$\frac{3}{8}$ of	$\frac{1}{2}$ of	$\frac{2}{3}$ of	40 % of	20 % of	75 % of	$\frac{1}{4}$ of
4 2	2 4	4 2	2 4	3 0	6 0	1 6	18 0
12 % of	$\frac{3}{4}$ of	75 % of	$\frac{1}{3}$ of	60 % of	$\frac{3}{4}$ of	$\frac{1}{3}$ of	2 % of
8 4	7 5	2 0	9 9	1 8	18 0	3 6	60 0

☐ + △ = ◯

☐ + △ = ◯

☐ + △ = ◯

☐ + △ = ◯

☐ + △ = ◯

☐ + △ = ◯

☐ + △ = ◯

☐ + △ = ◯

☐ + △ = ◯

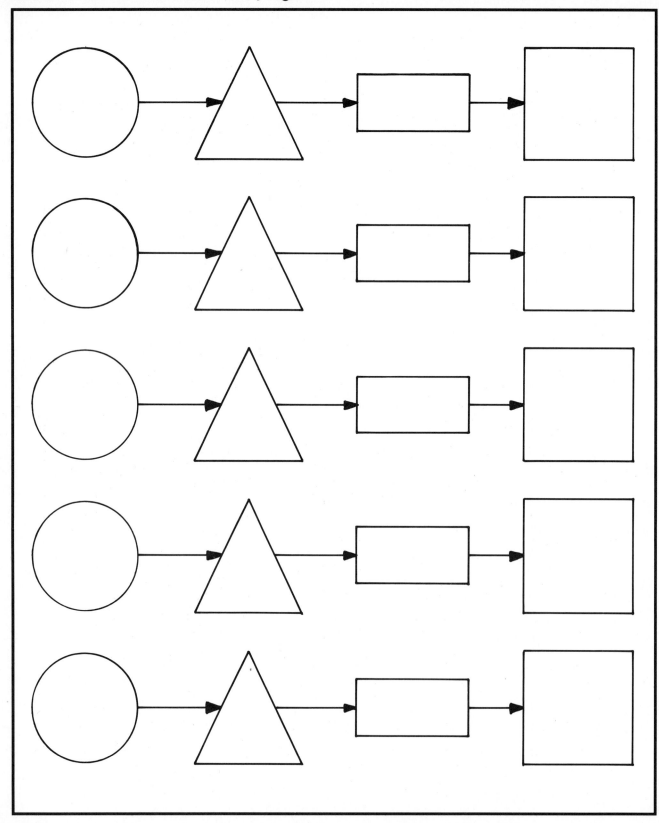

Number wall, page 42

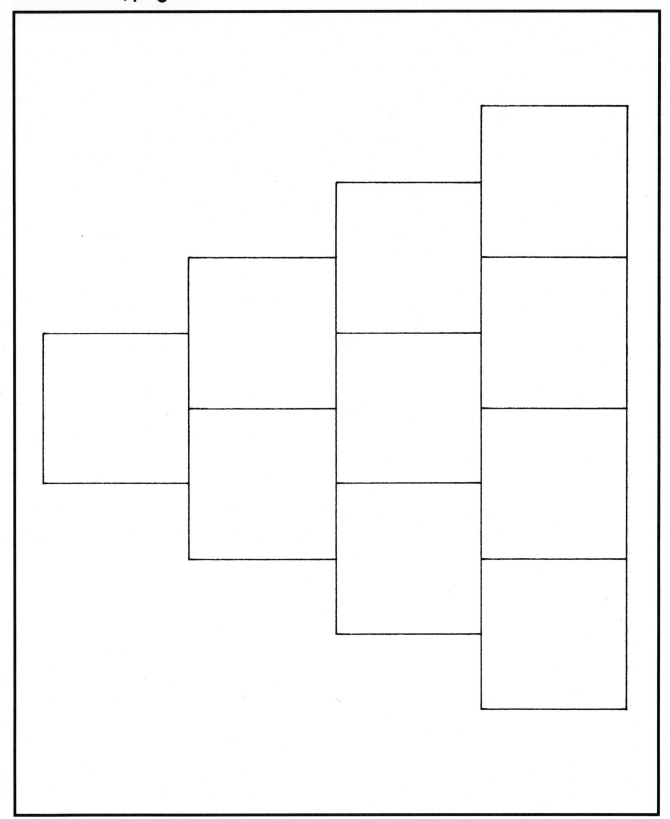

Profile of a favourite toy, page 48

Name:

Age:

Passport picture:

Colour of eyes:

Weight:

Profile of a favourite toy, page 48

Height:

Size of head:

Waist/tummy:

Length of arm:

Length of leg:

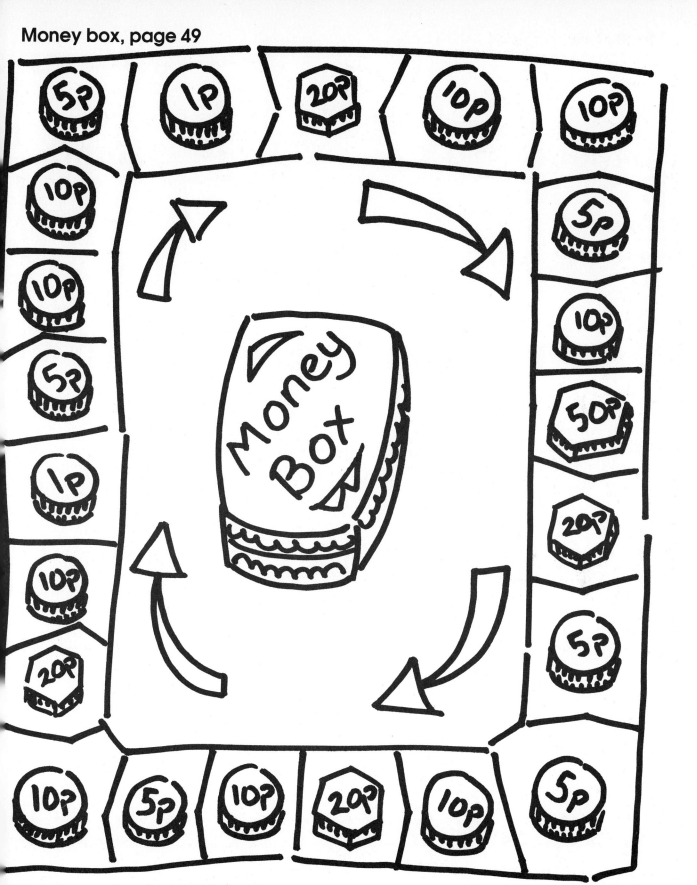

$\frac{1}{2}$ metre	0.5m	50cm	500mm
$\frac{1}{4}$ metre	0.25m	25cm	250mm
$\frac{3}{4}$ metre	0.75m	75cm	750mm
1 metre	1.0m	100cm	1000mm

$\frac{1}{2}$ litre	0.5l	50cl	500ml
$\frac{1}{4}$ litre	0.25l	25cl	250ml
$\frac{3}{4}$ litre	0.75l	75cl	750ml
1 litre	1.0l	100cl	1000ml

$\frac{1}{2}$ kg	0.5kg	500g	500,000mg
$\frac{1}{4}$ kg	0.25kg	250g	250,000mg
$\frac{3}{4}$ kg	0.75kg	750g	750,000mg
1kg	1.0kg	1000g	1,000,000mg

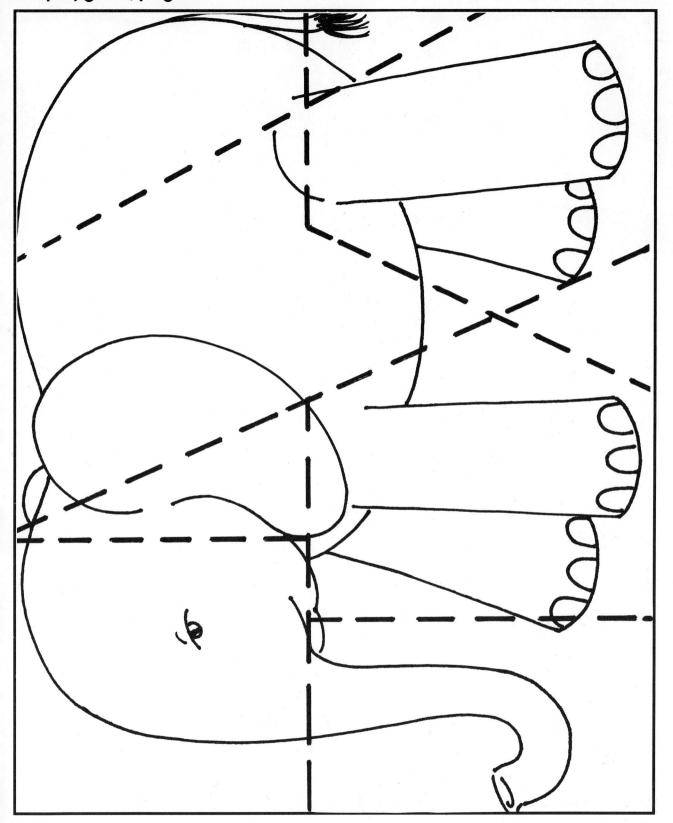

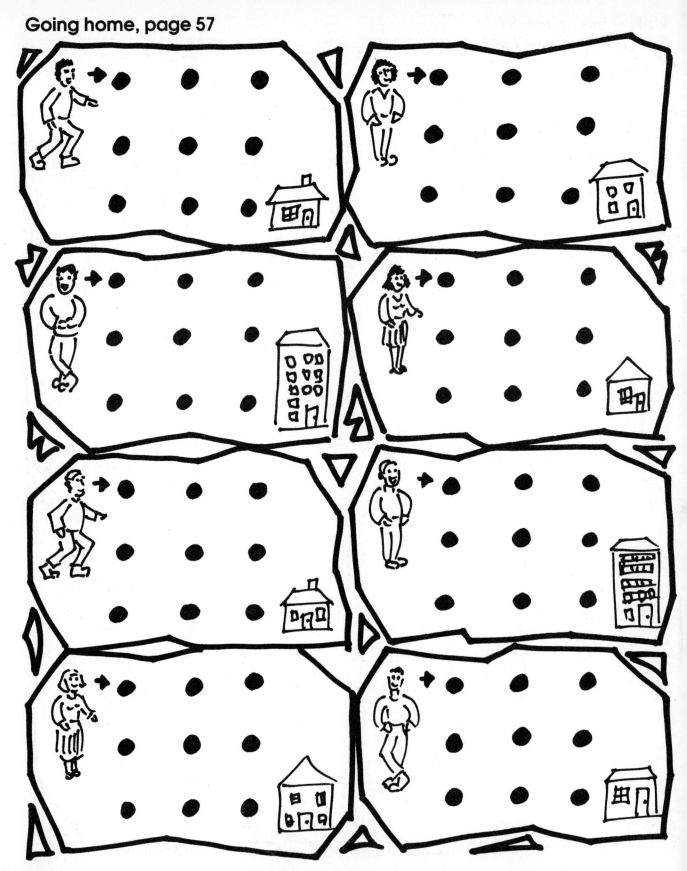

The supermarket, page 64

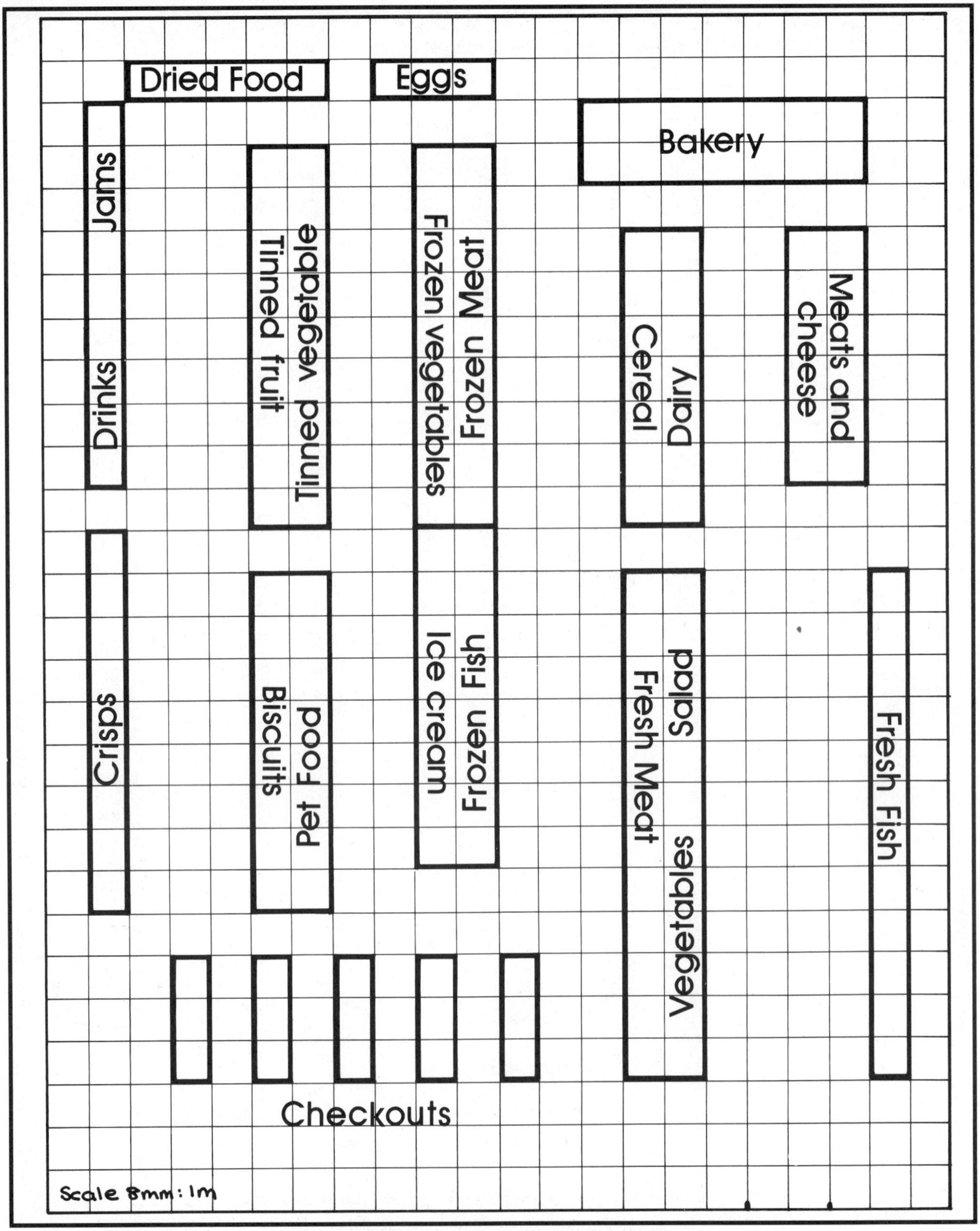

Dried Food
Eggs
Bakery
Jams
Drinks
Tinned vegetable
Tinned fruit
Frozen vegetables
Frozen Meat
Cereal
Dairy
Meats and cheese
Crisps
Biscuits
Pet Food
Ice cream
Frozen Fish
Fresh Meat
Salad
Vegetables
Fresh Fish
Checkouts
Scale 8mm : 1m

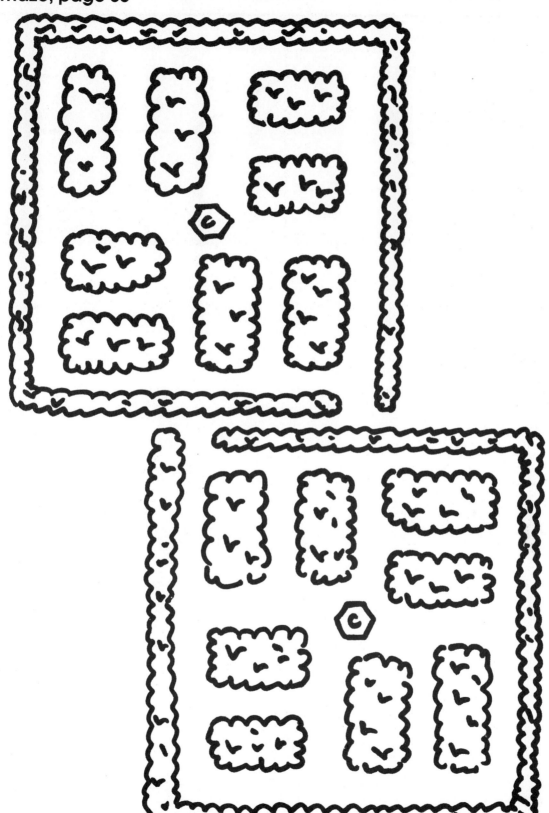

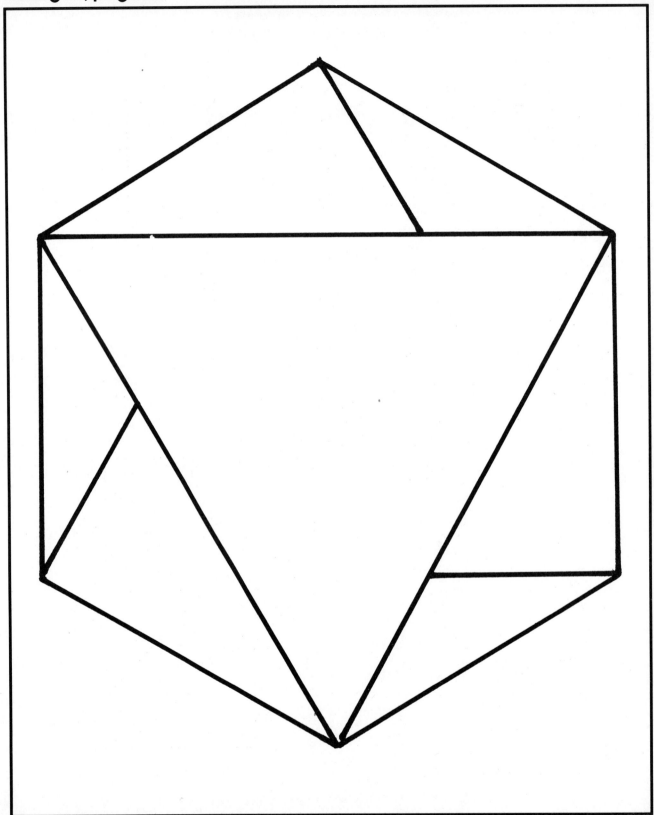

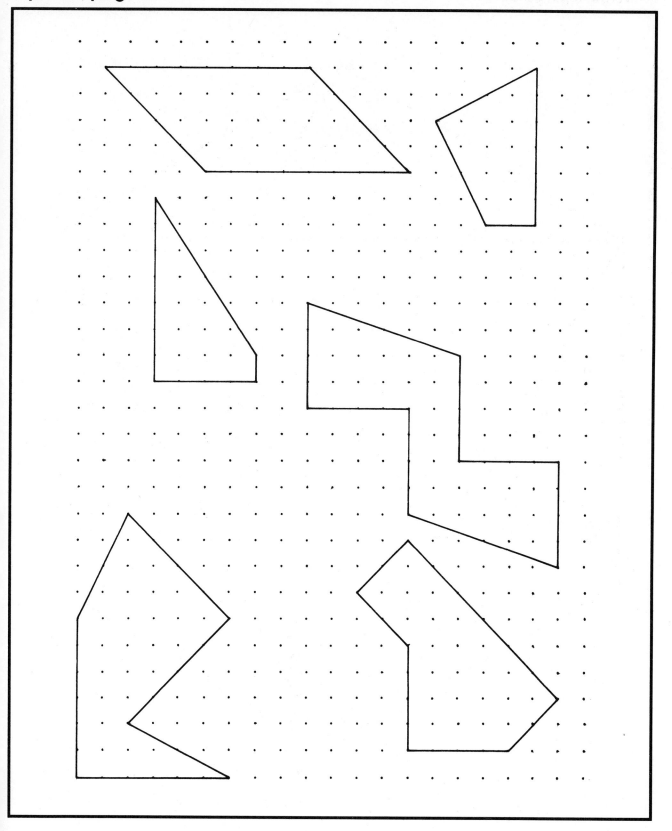

Girls are taller than boys.	All sides of an octagon are equal.	The number 6 is between 5 and 7.
A pint is more than a litre.	An hour is longer than a minute.	Two even numbers add up to an odd number.
Three 5p coins have a greater value than one 10p coin.	10 is half of 12.	May is before April.
There are 100g in a kilogram.	Days in summer are colder than days in winter.	A pentagon has 5 sides.

Tomorrow will be hot.	It will rain every day next week.
It will rain tomorrow.	It will snow on Sunday.
There will be a storm this month.	It will be dark by 9 o'clock tonight.
Tomorrow comes after today.	Tomorrow will be Sunday.

3	4	5
6	7	8
9	10	11

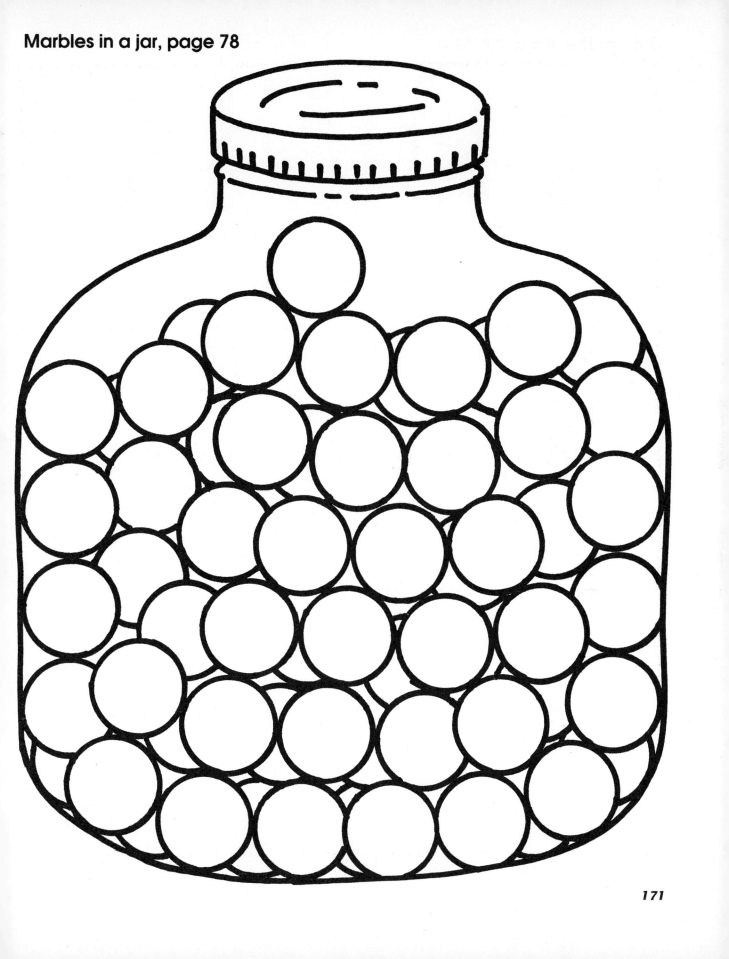

Rescue the cat, page 99

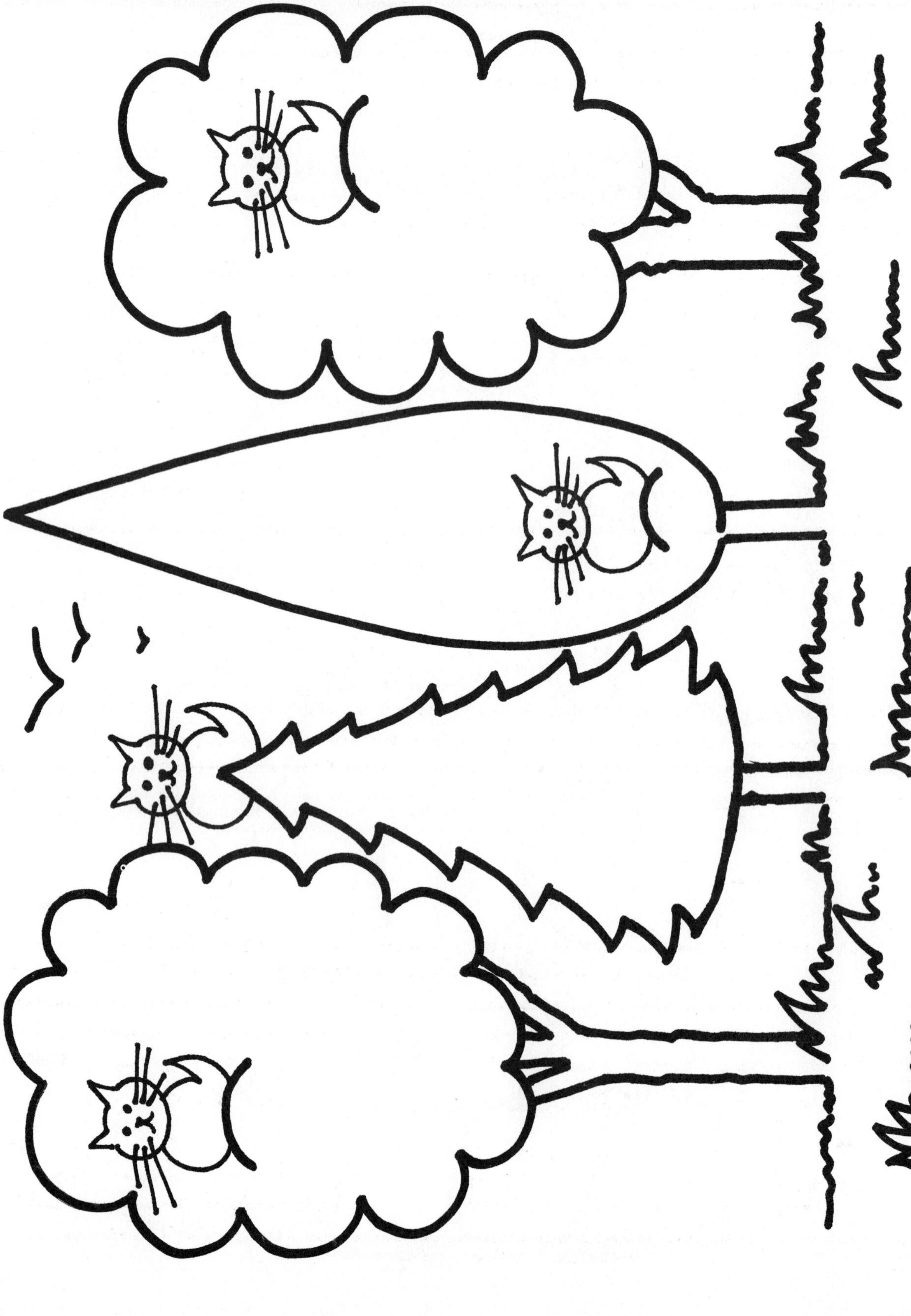

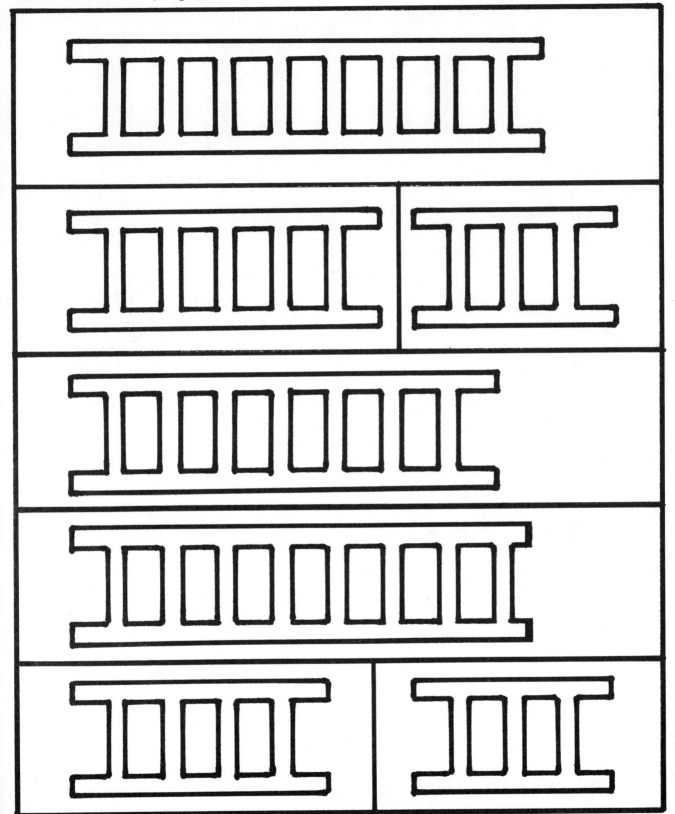

Rescue the cat, page 99

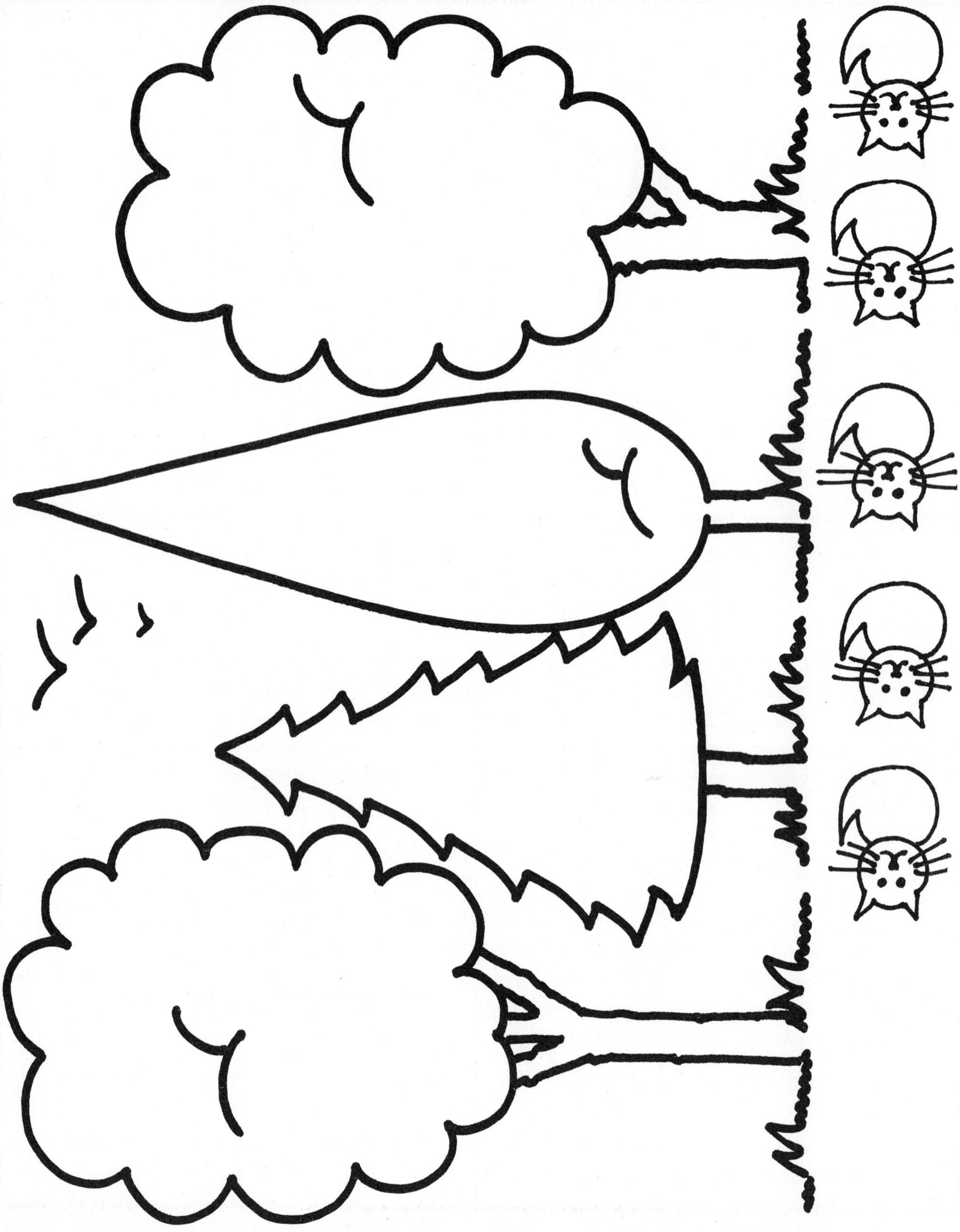

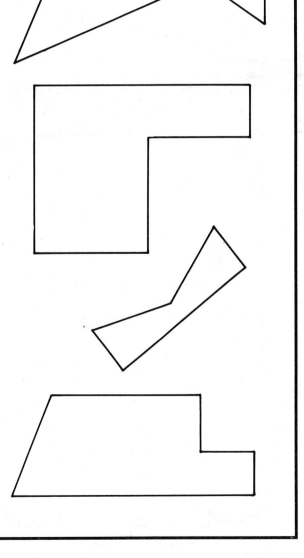

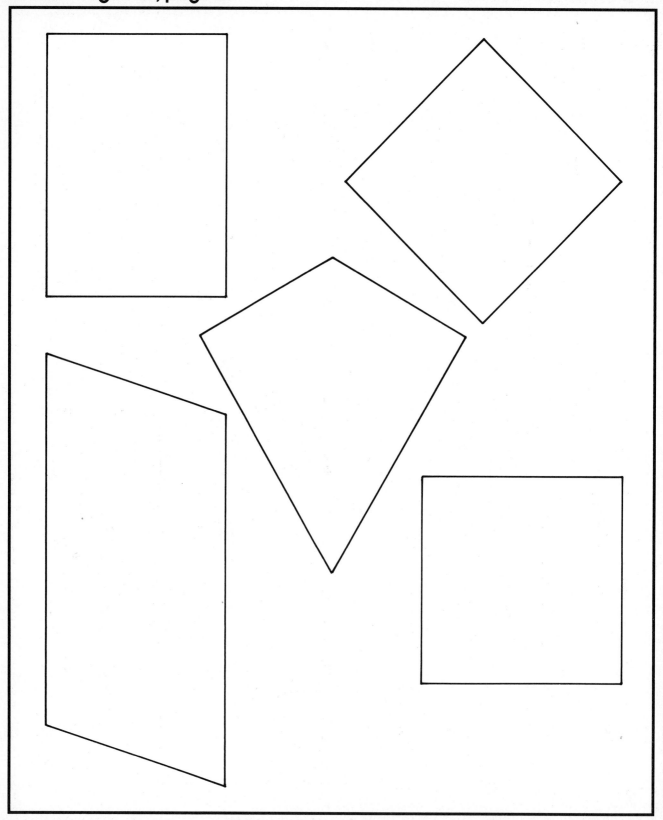

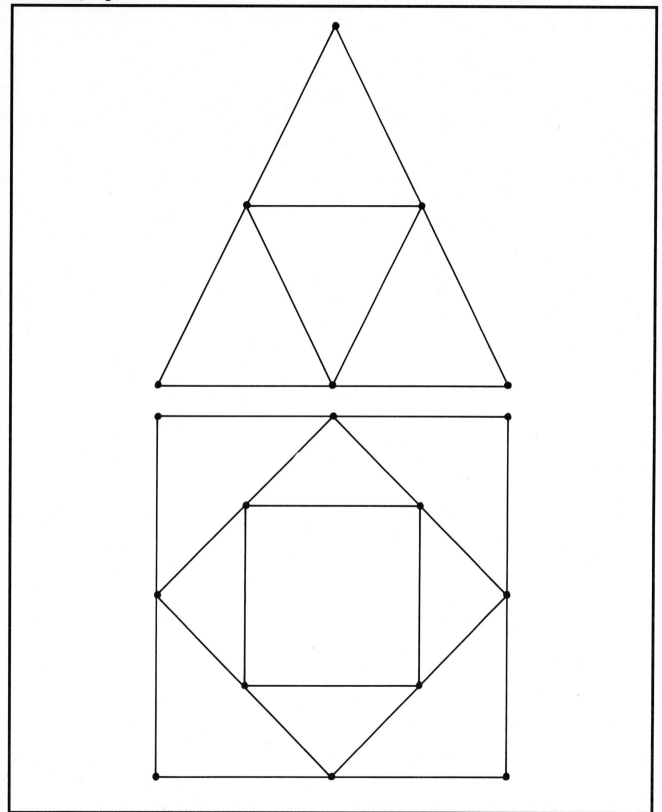

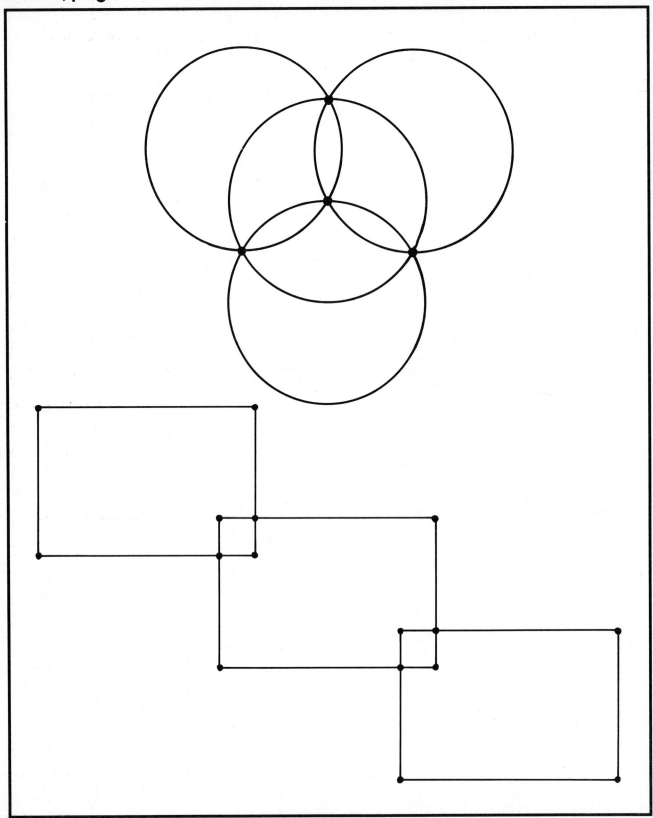

Record of planning, page 102

AT	AT2	AT3	AT4	AT5	AT6	AT7	AT8	AT10	AT11	AT12	AT13	AT14
Term 1												
Term 2												
Term 3												

	AT1							AT9				
Period 1	AT2	AT3	AT4	AT5	AT6	AT7	AT8	AT10	AT11	AT12	AT13	AT14
Period 2	AT2	AT3	AT4	AT5	AT6	AT7	AT8	AT10	AT11	AT12	AT13	AT14
Period 3	AT2	AT3	AT4	AT5	AT6	AT7	AT8	AT10	AT11	AT12	AT13	AT14
Period 4	AT2	AT3	AT4	AT5	AT6	AT7	AT8	AT10	AT11	AT12	AT13	AT14
Period 5	AT2	AT3	AT4	AT5	AT6	AT7	AT8	AT10	AT11	AT12	AT13	AT14
Period 6	AT2	AT3	AT4	AT5	AT6	AT7	AT8	AT10	AT11	AT12	AT13	AT14

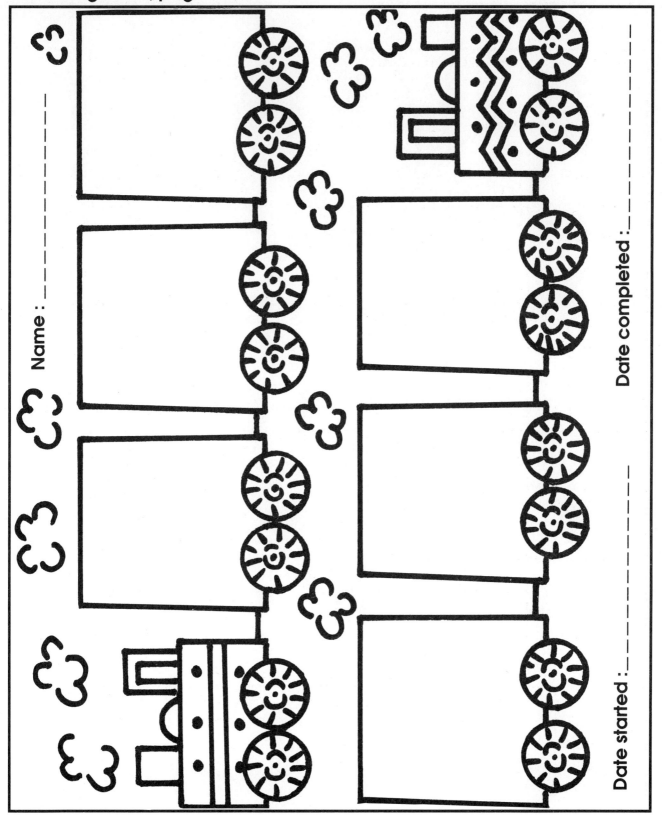

Name :

Date completed :

Date started :

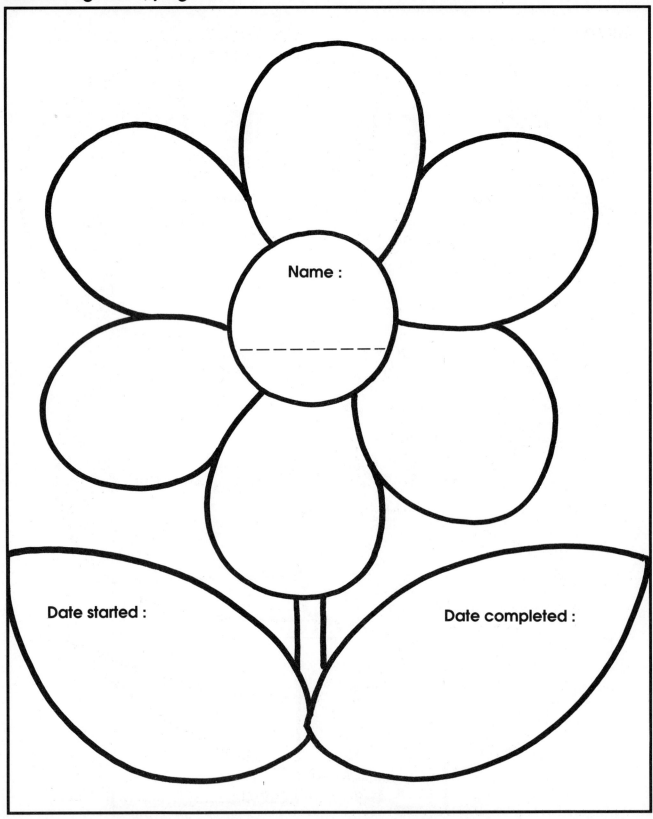

Name :

Date started :

Date completed :

Name : _____   Date started : _____

Date completed : _____

Recording chart, page 104

| 1 | 2 | 3 | 4 |

| 16 | | 5 |

Name:

_ _ _ _ _ _ _ _ _ _ _ _ _ _

| 15 | 6 |

Started:

_ _ _ _ _ _ _ _ _ _ _ _ _

| 14 | 7 |

Completed:

_ _ _ _ _ _ _ _ _ _ _ _ _

| 13 | 8 |

| 12 | 11 | 10 | 9 |

Name:

_ _ _ _ _ _ _ _

Term: _ _ _ _ _ _ _ _ _ _   Year: _ _ _ _ _ _ _ _ _ _

Recording assessment chart, page 108

Name:	Term:	Year:

Knowledge	
Concepts	
Skills	
Strategies	
Attitudes	

Recording assessment chart, page 108

Name:	Project:	Date:

What did you do and why?	
What surprised you?	
What did you find out?	
What mathematics did you use?	
What new mathematics did you learn?	

Framework for recording, page 109

	Level 1	Level 2	Level 3
Name:			
1			
2			
3			
4			
5			
6			
7			
8			
9			
10			
11			
12			
13			
14			

	Level 4	Level 5	Level 6
Name:			
1			
2			
3			
4			
5			
6			
7			
8			
9			
10			
11			
12			
13			
14			